002964

21.95
895

THE SPIRIT OF THE
TEN COMMANDMENTS

THE SPIRIT OF THE TEN COMMANDMENTS

Shattering the Myth of Rabbinic Legalism

ROGER BROOKS

1817

Harper & Row, Publishers, San Francisco

New York, Grand Rapids, Philadelphia, St. Louis
London, Singapore, Sydney, Tokyo, Toronto

FIRST EDITION

Library of Congress Cataloging-in-Publication Data

Brooks, Roger.
   The spirit of the Ten Commandments : shattering the myth of rabbinic legalism / Roger Brooks.—1st ed.
          p.   cm.
   Includes bibliographical references.
   ISBN 0-06-061132-4
   1. Ten commandments.   2. Jewish law—Philosophy.
3. Rabbinical literature—History and criticism.   I. Title.
BM520.75.B76   1990
296.1'8—dc20   89-45951
                                                                                CIP

90 91 92 93 94 HAD 10 9 8 7 6 5 4 3 2 1

For my father
Irving Brooks

Contents

Preface

Five years ago, I began teaching Judaic Studies at the University of Notre Dame, and embarked upon a fascinating adventure in Jewish-Christian relations. Together, my colleagues and I have planned conferences and symposia on various topics of mutual interest: Jewish and Christian liturgy, the aftermath of Vatican II, Israel as a Jewish State and as our joint Holy Land, and the *Shoah*, the Jewish Holocaust, which stands as an indictment of European anti-Semitism and calls into question any simple improvements in interfaith relations.

Over time, it became clear to me that when I spoke of Jewish law (*halakhah*), my students hardly understood my meaning. Some compared Jewish law to Catholic casuistry—certainly out of fashion these days—while others contrasted Jewish legalism with Christian spirituality. One of the most interesting challenges facing me, therefore, has been to explain Jewish law as a category, the purveyor of morality and ethics, as well as a deep spirituality, but thoroughly expressed in the legal details of day-to-day practice.

An understanding of the halakhic legal process in fact requires a full appreciation of the biblical foundation of rabbinic law. The rabbis of the early rabbinic movement sought within the Hebrew Bible a basis for all Jewish thought and opinion and understood this quest as effecting a return to Sinai and to God's revelation to Israel. Fundamental concepts and facts taken from that collection of Scriptures thus have formed the core of Judaic theology from the earliest times to our own day. But which set of ideas did the rabbis develop in a given circumstance? Which biblical facts did they emphasize? Such simple questions about the rabbis' development of antecedent Jewish law can tell much about the thought and views of those who interpreted the

Hebrew Bible and who saw themselves as guardians of God's truth.

This study explores early rabbinic Judaism's attitude toward biblical law: did the rabbis construct a system that attempted only to spell out the details and the letter of the biblical law, merely a literalistic and fundamentalistic legal review? Or, did rabbinic literature seek to move beyond legalism to determine the law's underlying principles and to construct a deeper hermeneutic, which we might call the spirit of the law?[1]

This problem is pressing, because bitter polemics have cast the image of Judaism as a strict legalist tradition, at least since the days of the New Testament. Anyone familiar with the highly charged interfamilial arguments advanced by early Christians against their Jewish roots might expect to find in the rabbinic movement a Pharisaic adherence to the letter of biblical law, one that bastardized the point of religious observance. Rather than paying attention to the true spirit of the Hebrew Scriptures, the legacy of Pharisaism would be seen as missing the point through its slavelike literalism.

Rabbinic Judaism, however, has always resisted such a polemical vision of its own legal system. In particular, the rabbis of the first four centuries of the Common Era asserted that true piety (qedushah, "holiness") emerged from advancing the law conceptually and intellectually. Rabbinic Judaism promoted the notion that study of the law (Talmud Torah) had a profound and beneficial impact upon the human mind. Furthermore, the discernment of enduring principles of behavior in the received tradition, coupled with the application of those principles to contemporary circumstances, likewise infused Jewish practice

---

1. "The spirit of the law" is of course most familiar from Montesquieu's political treatise, The Spirit of the Laws, English translation by Thomas Nugent (New York: Hafner Press, 1949; originally published 1748), which argues that law must be understood within the context of the underlying cultural climate from which it emerges. I use the term similarly to refer to the underlying theology of rabbinic law, captured in the Hebrew terms Torah—revelation—and halakhah—the way one leads a life of piety.

and behavior with a progressive edge. The law, as the rabbis understood and explained it, represented the spirit of God's revelation to the Jewish people at Sinai. The very act of participating in the legal system—an engagement that absorbed and lent sanctity to every moment of one's life—itself constituted the proper goal of religious practice.

In discussing this rabbinic attitude toward law, I shall focus on early Talmudic traditions from the Land of Israel concerning the Ten Commandments. The Ten Commandments are indigenously Jewish law, different formally from other Near Eastern legal codes, and standing at the foundation of the broader biblical system. The Ten Commandments constitute the centerpiece of the Sinaitic covenant and of God's revelation. These few verses, found in Exodus and repeated (with minor variations) in Deuteronomy, encapsulate the principal ethical and theological teachings of ancient Israel in legal discourse. So if we can determine how the rabbis interpreted and elaborated these imperatives, we will gain insight into their relation to biblical law as a whole. If the rabbis were mere literalists, we should see this in their interpretations of the Ten Commandments. Similarly, these materials will show us the underlying theory—the spirit—of Jewish law.

What image of the rabbinic legal system emerges from this study? For the rabbis, studying the law and uncovering ever-new layers of meanings constituted genuine piety. The rabbis contended, therefore, that study of the Decalogue—in fact of all biblical materials—might uncover the underlying rationale and purposes of Jewish law; such study represents the most vital act of the religious Jew. The rabbinic treatment of the Ten Commandments finds holiness in submission to rabbinic law as a system, to the rabbi as a sage, and to the entire corpus of rabbinic teaching, itself the ultimate object of study because of its status as God's ultimate gift to humankind.

Acknowledgments

Many colleagues provided useful counsel during my work on this book. I thank in particular John Collins (Department of Theology, University of Notre Dame), who encouraged this project from its earliest stages, as well as Elliot Bartky (Department of Political Science, Indiana University at Fort Wayne) and Michael Signer (Hebrew Union College-Jewish Institute of Religion, Los Angeles), both of whom took time from busy schedules to read the entire manuscript. These three friends encouraged and challenged me, and the book is vastly improved because of them. I owe a debt of collegiality as well to Joseph P. Bauer (University of Notre Dame Law School), Leslie Griffin (formerly of the Department of Theology, University of Notre Dame), David Levenson (Department of Religious Studies, Florida State University), and Tzvee Zahavy (Ancient Near Eastern and Jewish Studies, University of Minnesota) for their advice and suggestions. The influence of my teacher Jacob Neusner, who has pioneered a new agenda in Judaic studies, of course has been seminal throughout.

My thanks also are extended to Richard P. McBrien, Chairman of the Department of Theology, who enables the best possible work to be accomplished at Notre Dame. My gratitude goes as well to the University of Notre Dame itself, for its support through granting me research leave during 1988–1989, when this book was written.

Citations from the Hebrew Bible are taken from *TANAKH: The Holy Scriptures: The New JPS Translation according to the Traditional Hebrew Text* (Jewish Publication Society, 1988), and are used by permission. In order to provide a more egalitarian viewpoint, however, I have replaced male pronouns referring to the Deity (such as "His") with a bracketed reference (e.g., "[God's]" or "[the LORD's]").

This volume is lovingly dedicated to my father, Irving Brooks, for his consistent endorsement and encouragement. In all my teaching and research, his probing questions help shape my thoughts; this book is my gift of thanks to him.

Roger Brooks
June 9, 1989
6 *Sivan* 5749
The anniversary of God's revealing the Ten Commandments

1. The Spirit of Biblical Law

When Jews and Christians look back to the Hebrew Bible (also *Tanakh*, or Old Testament), they embrace a few short sentences in common that summarize their cultural values and religious beliefs. The Ten Commandments, the record of God's most basic guidance to the Israelite nation, undergird the Judeo-Christian tradition of law and ethics. They specify people's proper attitudes and behaviors toward one another as well as before their God. This sets forth a social and religious covenant important throughout Judaic, Christian, and Islamic civilizations everywhere. As found in Exodus 20:1–14, the Ten Commandments read:

God spoke all these words, saying:

I. I the Lord am your God who brought you out of the land of Egypt, the house of bondage.

II. You shall have no other gods besides Me. You shall not make for yourself a sculptured image, or any likeness of what is in the heavens above, or on the earth below, or in the waters under the earth. You shall not bow down to them or serve them. For I the Lord your God am an impassioned God, visiting the guilt of the parents upon the children, upon the third and upon the fourth generation of those who reject Me, but showing kindness to the thousandth generation of those who love Me and keep My commandments.

III. You shall not swear falsely by the name of the Lord your God; for the Lord will not clear one who swears falsely by [the Lord's] name.

IV. Remember the Sabbath day and keep it holy. Six days you shall labor and do all your work, but the seventh day is a Sabbath of the Lord your God: you shall not do any work—you, your son or daughter, your male or female slave, or your cattle, or the stranger who is within your settlements. For in six days the LORD made heaven and earth and sea, and all that is in them, and [the LORD] rested on the seventh day; therefore the LORD blessed the Sabbath day and hallowed it.

V. Honor your father and your mother, that you may long endure on the land that the LORD your God is assigning to you.

VI. You shall not murder.

VII. You shall not commit adultery.

VIII. You shall not steal.

IX. You shall not bear false witness against your neighbor.

X. You shall not covet your neighbor's house: you shall not covet your neighbor's wife, or his male or female slave, or his ox or his ass, or anything that is your neighbor's.[1]

The Ten Commandments: The Hebrew Bible's Legacy

The moral and theological guidance offered by the Ten Commandments is stirring. Upon reading the Decalogue, most people who have attended Sunday school at church or a Shabbat

---

1. The Decalogue is also found, with only slight variations, at Deut. 5:6–18. Here I follow the numeration scheme given by the Talmud of the Land of Israel, Berakhot 1:5 (see chapter 2 of this volume). Various other numeration schemes are possible, based in large measure on the Christian assertion that Exod. 20:3, "You shall have no other gods besides Me," forms an integral part of the first, not the second, command (see, for example, R. H. Charles, *The Decalogue* [Edinburgh: T. and T. Clark, 1923], pp. 1–13, who claims that Exod. 20:1–2 are wholly a later insertion). The New Oxford Annotated Bible, Revised Standard Version (New York: Oxford University Press, 1977), claiming to represent a broad consensus of biblical interpreters, in contrast to Jewish tradition, similarly accomplishes this shift by judging that "I am the LORD your God who brought you out of the land of Egypt, the house of bondage" is "actually . . . a preface that summarizes the meaning of the Exodus, thus setting law within the context of God's redemptive action" (see note to Exod. 20:2, p. 92). More recently, the Jewish Publication Society *TANAKH* places verse 3 at the conclusion of the first commandment, ascribing this numeration to a varying tradition. On the link between the First Commandment and the adjuration to eschew other gods, see chapter 4 of this volume.

morning program at synagogue would be moved to avoid these transgressions.

In the broad world of American politics, too, the Ten Commandments constitute the precious legacy of biblical literature. That is why President Jimmy Carter's admission "I have lusted in my heart" so nearly dealt a deathblow to his campaign; although Carter properly distinguished between intent and action, most Americans missed his subtlety, instead thinking that an issue so clearly religious and moral was an intrusion into the campaign. More recently, Gary Hart suffered in his presidential bid from his all-too-public violations of the Seventh Commandment, which prohibits adultery.

Legislative bodies also have recognized the essential quality of the Ten Commandments. Seeking to promote basic ethics contained in the Western tradition, a recent Kentucky statute required public schools to post a copy of the Ten Commandments prominently on the wall of each classroom in the state. At the bottom, in fine print, each display carried a justification for this inculcation within the public schools, normally purveyors of secular culture: "The secular application of the Ten Commandments is clearly seen in its adoption as the fundamental legal code of Western Civilization and the Common Law of the United States."

In due time, of course, the Supreme Court overturned the Kentucky law as an unconstitutional violation of the Establishment Clause of the First Amendment.[2] While this juridical defeat no doubt troubled a good many well-intentioned Kentuckians, they need not have worried about the indoctrination of children regarding the Ten Commandments. The mass media in the United States, from television and film to print, place the Ten Commandments squarely in the public eye as part of popular culture. By the time we reach maturity, the Decalogue

---

2. See *Stone et al.* v. *Graham, Superintendent of Public Instruction of Kentucky* (449 U.S. 39).

simply resides in our educational background, ready to come forth at the slightest calling. Even a glimpse at a stark line drawing of the Tablets serves as a potent mnemonic aid.

Immediately upon seeing such a depiction, we think of right and wrong, of parental honor and Sabbath, of idolatry and adultery. In fact, for most Westerners, the mere representation of the Tablets provides instant meaning and context. Because of the immediacy of our understanding, a remarkable range of references to the Ten Commandments is possible. Above the pulpit, many synagogues place hewn tablets, marked only with ten Roman numerals, yet everyone understands the reference perfectly clearly. Even a satirist's cartoon can play on our knowledge, invoked merely by a bearded old man holding the Stone Tablets.

This joke is funny—in fact it is recognizable as a joke—only because of our intimate understanding of "this stuff." Because of the Ten Commandments' prominence in our traditions, we immediately supply God's revelation at Mount Sinai and the prohibition against adultery as the context for the remark.

If the Ten Commandments are central to Judeo-Christian culture, however, the endorsement is not one hundred percent. The Ten Commandments, after all, place the principal ethical teachings of ancient Israel in *legal* form. They reduce morality to mere rules of law, and law and obligation have not been popular within Christian biblical scholarship in modernity.

In fact, scholars have tended to read the entire Hebrew Bible, especially the Pentateuch, as a legalistic document. That is to say, the Bible portrays a God of judgment and punishment, who scrupulously attends to how well the people of Israel toe the line laid down through the Decalogue and the rest of the Sinaitic law and covenant. The Bible may speak of grand themes—creation, monotheism, theodicy, and others—but it does so in the most detailed discussions of law: laws governing worship; laws governing the monarchy; laws governing the sacrificial cult; laws governing every detail of Israelite life. This rather condescending view of biblical literature has shaped our attitudes toward all religious law. But Judaism in particular— the religion par excellence—has suffered at the hands of biblical scholars.[3]

This depiction of legalistic Judaism is most cogently expressed in the writings of Julius Wellhausen, particularly his

"If this stuff is retroactive to last weekend, we're in big trouble."

---

3. See David Hartmann, *A Living Covenant: The Innovative Spirit in Traditional Judaism* (New York: Free Press, 1985), pp. 1–4.

Prolegomenon to the History of Ancient Israel.[4] In his deliberations on the formation of the Bible's many books, Wellhausen developed a historical scheme leading from simple Mosaic piety to the heights of prophetic monotheism. But according to Wellhausen, Judaism as we know it, in its legal (and later rabbinic) manifestation, emerged during the decline and fall of ancient Israelite society. This decline, which followed the Babylonian exile and return in the late sixth century B.C.E., was caused by an overabundant focus on the main institution of communal life, the Temple cult, and on law to regulate that institution. In this necessary (and regrettable) shift in communal focus, Wellhausen argued, Israel changed from a people led by prophets to a nation led by priests. Such leadership "transformed their spiritual point of view into a legalistic preoccupation with the ritual laws of worship."[5]

Wellhausen's concept of *Spätjudentum*—late Judaism—is best illustrated through the legalism of the priestly author of Leviticus, believed to have edited the entire Pentateuch.[6] Using a

---

4. Wellhausen, *Prolegomenon to the History of Ancient Israel. With a Reprint of the Article "Israel," from the Encyclopedia Britannica. Preface by W. Robertson Smith* (Gloucester, Mass.: Peter Smith Publisher, 1973; originally published 1886), pp. 52–58, 99–108,164–70, 376–91, and 402–8. For a discussion of this theme in German biblical scholarship and of Wellhausen's dependence upon Wilhelm M. L. de Wette, see Rolf Rendtorff, "The Image of Post-Exilic Israel in German Bible Scholarship from Wellhausen to von Rad," delivered at the 1988 Annual Meeting of the Society of Biblical Literature, Chicago, Illinois.
5. Herbert F. Hahn, *The Old Testament in Modern Research: With a Survey of Recent Literature by Horace D. Hummel* (Philadelphia, Pa.: Fortress Press, 1966), p. 14.
6. In discussing the formulation of Pentateuchal traditions, Wellhausen carried forward seminal work by Karl H. Graf and others, showing by the mid-1860s that four separate documents together comprised the Pentateuch, the latest of which was written by a priest in the fifth century B.C.E. While many modern Jewish thinkers accept this basic premise, a refutation of the Documentary Hypothesis, consistent with traditional Judaic theology, may be found in Umberto Cassuto, *La Questione della Genesi* (Florence: Publicazioni della R. Università degli Studi di Firenze. Facoltà di Lettere e Filosofia, 3d series, vol. 1, 1934), later revised and issued as *The Documentary Hypothesis and the Composition of the Pentateuch* (Jerusalem: Magnes Press, 1961; originally published in Hebrew, 1941), cf. esp. pp. 98–105. See also Jon D. Levenson,

solemn, repetitive style, full of stereotypical idioms and a perfect balance of structure, the "Priestly Writer" was more interested in symmetry than in storytelling. So, Wellhausen held, the Priestly Writer turned his back on earlier, more picaresque and evocative stories told by the Jerusalemite author who penned the imaginative tales of God's gracious relationship with Abraham and his family. As far as Wellhausen was concerned, this shift to a nation in the late sixth century B.C.E. marked the overall degradation of biblical Israel from the heights of prophecy to mere law, and from a free, spontaneously religious people to a Temple-bound cult.

In discussing and reviling "Old Testament Law," Wellhausen's school eventually gave rise to a clever distinction. In 1934, the German biblical scholar Albrecht Alt sought to separate two types of biblical law. The first category of law closely resembled rules from other law codes of the ancient Middle East, whether Babylonian, Assyrian, or Hittite. These portions of biblical law embodied a thoroughly secular spirit, without religious or humanitarian basis. And their casuistic tone made it clear that this was customary law, the normal juridical activity of local courts making and enforcing rules. The second category of law Alt deemed natively Hebrew, due to its solemn tone and uncompromising cast. "In contrast to casuistic law, [this apodictic law] embodied generalized principles covering the most important aspects of ethical life rather than specific regulations dealing with a multitude of practical eventualities."[7]

For Alt and the "form critics" who followed his lead, casuistic law was to be devalued in regard to apodictic law. In the first place, the authorizing body standing behind casuistic law was merely the local judiciary. Since such law arose from real jurisprudence, it was tainted by the exigencies of everyday life. Apodictic regulations, by contrast, were created not to meet

Sinai and Zion: An Entry into the Jewish Bible (Minneapolis, Minn.: Winston Press, 1985), pp. 4–11.

7. Hahn, *Old Testament in Modern Research*, p. 148.

legislative goals, but to embody the beliefs and values of the entire religious community. These laws were rooted in a ceremonial recitation of communal values. Apodictic regulations thus were not "law" as such, but theology native to God's chosen people. Furthermore, Judaism in its rabbinic formulation (à la Wellhausen's *Spätjudentum*) fostered the casuistic laws, adding detail and specification to each possible circumstance in biblical law. Given this "spiritually bankrupt" religion's embrace, it is little wonder that Christians broadly—and Protestant biblical scholars in particular—rejected casuistic law as lifeless and wooden.

On the other hand, a distinction such as Alt's *did* serve to rescue the Ten Commandments, within Christian tradition, from charges of legalism. The Decalogue represented apodictic theology at its best, capturing the depths of God's interaction with the Israelites. Even while deprecating Judaism's legalism, Christians thus have been able to afford the Ten Commandments a privileged place as ethics and dogma.

But Wellhausen and Alt, characteristic of many Christian biblical scholars, missed the deeper reality of the Pentateuch's multivalenced law.[8] True, by examining portions of the Hebrew Bible in isolation, as for example the Covenant Code (Exod. 20–23), the Holiness Code (Lev. 17–26), and the Deuteronomic Code (Deut. 12–26), we see a marked tendency toward legal— even casuistic—expression.[9] Much of the Pentateuch utilizes case law rather than absolute prohibition to express its underlying message. Yet despite such legal form and structure, these codes of biblical law are embedded in a narrative structure that

---

8. Again, see Rendtorff, "Image of Post-Exilic Israel," for the legacy of Wellhausen's conceptions within German biblical scholarship. See also George Foot Moore, "Christian Writers on Judaism" in *Harvard Theological Review* 14, no. 3 (1921): esp. 228–36.
9. On biblical law, see Rolf Rendtorff, *The Old Testament: An Introduction* (Philadelphia, Pa.: Fortress Press, 1985; originally published in German, 1983), pp. 86–104; Lawrence Boadt, *Reading the Old Testament: An Introduction* (New York: Paulist Press, 1984), pp. 173–94.

itself helps generate their meaning. Furthermore, the law codes do not confine themselves to endless details of worship rites, but balance both "ritual" and "spiritual" materials. Alongside Levitical regulations on the cult, for example, we read Leviticus' own rules for social harmony (see especially Lev. 19). Similarly, Deuteronomy's legalistic framework for the inheritance of property when an Israelite dies without a male heir (a rite called levirate marriage, Deut. 25:5–10) is best understood through the narrative application found in the rather charming marriage proposal Boaz offered Ruth after her husband had passed away (Ruth 3:10–13, 4:3–15). So while the expression of the Pentateuch is largely casuistic, its substance, and that of the entire Hebrew Bible, runs the full gamut from ritual and cultic law on through to ethical and moral topics.

A cursory appeal to Judaic interpretations of the Pentateuchal materials bears out the observation that the Hebrew Bible's topics and interest range widely. Medieval Jewish biblical commentators, following the rabbis of Late Antiquity, asserted that the Hebrew Bible strove to balance two quite different images of the one God: the first image showed God as a legal and judgmental sovereign; the second portrayed God as a merciful parent. The most famous of all medieval rabbinic commentators, Rashi (southern France, 1040–1105 C.E.),[10] wrote that the biblical text provided literary clues regarding these two complementary images: when the text refers to God as "the LORD" (using the Tetragrammaton, YHVH), the depiction tends toward the God of mercy. And when the Bible refers merely to "God" (using the more generic Hebrew "Elohim"), the passage at hand tends to show God's aspect of strict judgment.[11]

Far earlier Talmudic traditions also dealt with the balance within the Deity between justice and mercy, between legalism

---

10. For details of Rashi's life and oeuvre, see Esra Shereshevsky, *Rashi: The Man and His Life* (New York: Sepher-Hermon Press, 1982).

11. See Rashi's commentary to Gen. 1:1 in Abraham Berliner, ed., *Rashi on the Torah*, 2nd rev. ed. (Frankfurt am Main: Kaufmann, 1905), p. 1.

and morality. The following excerpt from the Talmud of the Land of Israel (ca. 450 C.E.) explicitly establishes God's strict reward and punishment of one's actions, whether good or evil. Having established a correspondence between God's judgments and the underlying human actions, the Talmud then spells out the true nature of divine mercy: God inclines ever so slightly toward the benefit of Israelite subjects.

Yerushalmi Peah 1:1 [Venice: 16b; Vilna: 5a]

One who performs mostly good deeds inherits the Garden of Eden, and one who performs mostly transgressions inherits *Gehenna*. [But what if the scales] are balanced, [so that the person has neither a majority of sins nor a majority of good deeds]?

Said R. Yose b. Hanina, "[Consider Exod. 34:6–7's description of God's attributes]; *'Who forgives transgressions'* [in the plural] is not written there, but rather, *'Who forgives transgression'* [in the singular]. [This means that] the Holy, Blessed One will seize one document [bearing the record of one of] a person's transgressions, so that the good deeds will outweigh [the transgressions]."

Said R. Eleazar, "And unto you, O LORD, belongs mercy, for You pay each person according to his or her works. But if a person has no good deeds, you give one of Your own." This is the opinion of R. Eleazar. For R. Eleazar said, "[Exod. 34:6–7 describes God as having] *'much mercy'*—that is, [God] tips the scale toward mercy, [even to the point of giving evil doers credit for good deeds they never performed]."[12]

Such a passage points up the rabbis' belief in the diversity of the tradition they inherited through biblical literature. In the rabbis' theological judgment, neither the judgmental nor the merciful aspect of God utterly predominated. Both judgment and mercy, law and spirit, infused the legal tradition, although

---

12. Translation from Roger Brooks, *The Talmud of the Land of Israel: A Preliminary Translation and Commentary,* vol. 2, *Tractate Peah* (Chicago, Ill.: University of Chicago Press, 1990), p. 76. For a parallel passage, see B. Rosh Hashanah 17a.

in the slightest measure mercy had the upper hand. This gives an important clue to the early rabbinic attitude toward Judaic legalism. Already by the early fifth century we see the rabbis softening a literal reading of transgression and punishment; already we find attention to the problematic relationship between law and spirit. Yet the legalistic vision of Judaism persists, and we must not allow the *formal* legalism of Pentateuchal and Judaic theology to eclipse the multifaceted *content* of God's revelation.

The Letter of the Law

Despite arguments that Judaism is not merely a religion of legalism and literalism, scholars have often drawn a facile contrast between the Hebrew Bible and the New Testament, in which the latter is seen to portray a religious movement of love and mercy.[13] Now, there *are* important differences between the Hebrew Bible and the New Testament, for example, the legal expression of the former—found within the context of a narrative tradition—as against the more purely narrative character of the latter. Jewish legal thought and expression *is* unlike Christian religious expression, and this difference is reflected

---

13. Classic discussions of this persistent view are found in James Barr, *The Bible in the Modern World* (San Francisco, Calif.: Harper & Row, 1973), pp. 164–67, and E. P. Sanders, *Paul and Palestinian Judaism: A Comparison of Patterns of Religion* (Philadelphia, Pa.: Fortress Press, 1977), pp. 33–59. More traditional reviews of Christian thought on the relationship between the Hebrew Bible and New Testament are found in D. L. Baker, *Two Testaments, One Bible: A Study of Some Modern Solutions to the Theological Problem of the Relationship of the Old and New Testaments* (Leicester, England: Inter-Varsity Press, 1976), esp. pp. 179–81, 224, 284–85, and 372–74. See also Albert Vanhoye, *Old Testament Priests and the New Priest, According to the New Testament* (Petersham, Mass.: St. Bede's Publications, 1986; originally published in French, 1980), pp. xi–xv, 164–67; and Morna Dorothy Hooker, *New Wine in Old Bottles: A Discussion of Continuity and Discontinuity in Relation to Judaism and the Gospels*, The 1984 Ethel M. Wood Trust Lecture (London: London University Press, 1984), p. 18.

in the biblical motifs used in the New Testament and in early rabbinic literature.

The New Testament highlights what has been called the "David-Zion" motif.[14] This biblical pattern involves God's unconditional promise of support for the Israelite people, through and because of a single ruler descended from King David and reigning over the Temple cult in Jerusalem. Found throughout parts of the patriarchal narratives in Genesis, in the promises of 2 Samuel, in the prophetic work of Isaiah, and throughout the Psalms, this pattern of perpetual security and Davidic monarchy enabled the emerging Christian movement to find the origins of the Christ story in the Hebrew Scriptures. Jesus embodied God's unconditional love for the people; Jesus was a lineal descendant from the Davidic house; Jesus was proclaimed king of the Jews in Zion; and if some New Testament writings tended to de-emphasize Jesus' role as a Davidic figure, they nonetheless highlighted the Temple cult, continued on in the person of Jesus himself—the embodiment of the perfect sacrifice and the perfect high priest. Because Christianity focused solely on the completely unconditional nature of Gods' promise within this David-Zion motif, it is no surprise that the New Testament authors were able to abandon adherence to a strict legal code. And while proper behavior did play a prominent role, especially in the Pauline letters, such moral exhortations rarely approached true legal mandates.[15]

Rabbinic Judaism, for its part, stressed a theme from the Hebrew Bible that modern scholars have termed the "Moses-Sinai"

---

14. For this motif in the Hebrew Bible, see, for example, John Bright, *A History of Israel*, 3d ed. (Philadelphia, Pa.: Westminster Press, 1981), pp. 224–25. See also Levenson, *Sinai and Zion*, pp. 187–217.

15. See, e.g., Gal. 6:1–10; 1 Thess. 5:12–28. See also Victor Paul Furnish, *Theology and Ethics in Paul* (Nashville, Tenn.: Abingdon, 1968), pp. 68–111; E. P. Sanders, *Paul, the Law, and the Jewish People* (Philadelphia, Pa.: Fortress Press, 1983), pp. 143–49, on the exhortation as a quasi-legal form. See also Robert L. Wilken, *The Christians as the Romans Saw Them* (New Haven, Conn.: Yale University Press, 1984), p. 22, for Pliny's summary of Christian practice largely within a legal (and Decalogue-centered) framework.

motif.[16] This theme is represented in the Sinai cycle of Exodus, as well as in the stories of the Northern Kingdom of Israel found in the books of Kings and throughout the prophetic visions of Amos and Hosea. The main focus of the Moses-Sinai motif is on the lawgiver, Moses, and on the covenant God established through him at Mount Sinai. This motif accurately reflected the contingent nature of God's protection over Israel. God gave the people a set of rules for daily life, worship, and foreign relations, and would support the Israelites when the rules were upheld. Disaster and national crisis would occur, by contrast, if Israel failed to follow God's mandates. Given the rabbis' belief in this quid pro quo, we can more easily understand their attention to the most minute details of law. They wished to spell out as clearly as possible the manner in which Jews ought to carry out their lives so as to assure God's merciful and gracious protection. Nonetheless, the rabbis never assumed that chastisement from God meant the abrogation of the covenant. In fact, the distinctions between the eternal Davidic promise and the more conditional Sinaitic covenant did not render them mutually exclusive, except in the radical Christian critique of Judaism.

The sharp divergence between Judaism and Christianity emerged when rabbinic Judaism continued to emphasize God's demands upon Israel, while the early Christian writers, believing that the law had been fulfilled with the coming of Jesus, chose to highlight the story of God's unconditional and unending support, now manifest in a new covenant of grace. And the patristic writers, who continued to develop Christian theology from the mid–second century on through to the sixth and seventh centuries, sharpened the Christian critique of Judaism. Notably, the anti-Judaic movement (*Adversus Judaeos*) spanned

---

16. For a slightly different formulation of these alternative Christian and Jewish motifs, see Michael Goldberg, *Jews and Christians: Getting Our Stories Straight: The Exodus and the Passion-Resurrection* (Nashville, Tenn.: Abingdon Press, 1985).

most all of Christendom, from the Iranian monk Aphrahat (fl. 300–350 C.E.) in the eastern Syriac Christian tradition, to the Bishop John Chrysostom (fl. 349–400 C.E.) in Antioch, and even to Roman African communities represented, for example, by Tertullian (fl. 160–220 C.E.).[17] Important studies have shown the extent to which leaders of the early church lambasted Judaism for its slavish adherence to the letter of the law,[18] particularly through simple claims that Christ had fulfilled and thereby eliminated all law secondary to the Ten Commandments, and that Judaism henceforth would continue to exist primarily as an example of degradation. The early third-century leader of the Palestinian Christian community in Caesarea, Origen, summed up the difference between Jewish and Christian approaches to Scripture in a manner representative of the entire patristic corpus, although he lacks something of the virulent invective of his colleagues.

It seems necessary also to explain how certain people by failing to read or understand Scripture correctly have given themselves up to a great many errors, since the way one ought to approach the understanding of divine letters is unknown to a great many people. And so, the Jews, through the hardness of their heart and because they wish to seem wise in themselves, have not believed in our Lord and Savior. . . .

Now the reason that those we have just mentioned [Jews and heretical Christians] have a false understanding of these matters is quite simply that they understand Scripture not according to the *spiritual* meaning but according to the sound of the *letter*. . . .

17. See Robert L. Wilken, *John Chrysostom and the Jews: Rhetoric and Reality in the Late Fourth Century* (Berkeley: University of California Press, 1983); Jacob Neusner, *Aphrahat and Judaism: The Christian-Jewish Argument in Fourth-Century Iran* (Leiden: E.J. Brill, 1971); and Robert Wilde, *The Treatment of the Jews in the Greek Christian Writers of the First Three Centuries* (Washington, D.C.: Catholic University of America Press, 1949).
18. See John G. Gager, *The Origins of Anti-Semitism: Attitudes toward Judaism in Pagan and Christian Antiquity* (New York: Oxford University Press, 1983); Marcel Simon, *Verus Israel: A Study of the Relationships between Christians and Jews in the Roman Empire* (New York: Oxford, 1986; originally published in French, 1948).

[But] a person ought to describe threefold in his soul the meaning of divine letters, that is, so that the simple may be edified by, so to speak, *the body of the Scriptures;* for that is what we call the ordinary and narrative meaning. But if any have begun to make some progress and can contemplate something more fully, they should be edified by *the soul of Scripture.* And those who are perfect . . . should be edified by that spiritual Law (cf. Rom. 7:14) which has a shadow of the good things to come (cf. Heb. 10:1), edified by *the spirit of Scripture.* Thus, just as a human being is said to be made up of body, soul, and spirit, so also is sacred Scripture, which has been granted by God's gracious dispensation for man's salvation.[19]

This type of tripartite scheme for reading Scripture—and the assertion that Jews miss all but the literal meaning—makes for potent apologetics. The patristic dichotomy between "letter" and "spirit"—that is, between reading biblical materials either at face value as norms of behavior, or at some remove as indicators of a more generalized stance toward the world—set the stage throughout Christian history for an ever stronger charge of legalism.[20] The legacy of the *Adversus Judaeos* tradition still shapes many of our thoughts regarding Judaic law.

But without a much clearer picture of the actual workings of Jewish legal interpretation, we are left merely with polemics and the problems they have caused throughout history. For throughout Jewish history, interpretation of Scripture has been a multileveled enterprise.

In Late Antiquity, during the first four centuries of the rabbinic movement, the rabbis saw themselves as the true interpretive community, in contrast to all others who read and interpreted the Hebrew Bible, including early Christians, those

---

19. Origen, *On First Principles*, 4.2.1–4; translation from Rowan A. Greer, ed., *Origen*, Classics of Western Spirituality (New York: Paulist Press, 1979), p. 182.
20. In early Reformation thinkers, the legalism charge was part of a larger critique of Catholicism, which was held to have Judaized Christianity; Luther and Calvin, by contrast, claimed to be merely returning to the true spirit of the divine message.

who wrote the Dead Sea Scrolls, or even the Alexandrian communities represented, for example, in the writings of Philo. Yet this assertion that they were the only true interpreters of the Bible—i.e., that only they understood the legacy of Jewish law—did not translate into a claim that Scripture had but one meaning. Much of early rabbinic biblical commentary is found in a genre of writing known as *midrash*. *Midrash* is marked by a characteristic reading of Scripture as if it addressed the immediate circumstance of the rabbis themselves,[21] changeable and mutable as those settings surely were, and by its ability to spin out seemingly endless (and often contradictory) meanings based upon a single word or phrase of the underlying biblical text.[22] But for the rabbis,

the citation of multiple interpretations in *midrash* is an attempt to represent in textual terms an idealized academy of Rabbinic tradition where all the opinions of the sages are recorded equally as part of a single divine conversation. Opinions that in human discourse may appear as contradictory or mutually exclusive are raised to the state of paradox, once traced to their common source in the speech of the divine author. . . . Polysemy in *midrash*, then, is to be understood as a claim to textual stability, rather than its opposite, an indeterminate state of endlessly deferred meanings and unresolved conflicts.[23]

Such midrashic approaches differ from their patristic counterparts in so far as they offer truly multiple meanings of a

---

21. See, for example, Jacob Neusner, *Comparative Midrash: The Plan and Program of Genesis and Leviticus Rabbah* (Atlanta, Ga.: Scholars Press, 1986), pp. 139–41, 173–75.

22. See Judah Goldin, "From Text to Interpretation and from Experience to Interpreted Text," in *Studies in Midrash and Related Literature* (Philadelphia, Pa.: Jewish Publication Society, 1988), pp. 271–81, esp. p. 274. See also Jacob Neusner, *Mekhilta according to Rabbi Ishmael: An Introduction to Judaism's First Scriptural Encyclopaedia* (Atlanta, Ga.: Scholars Press, 1988), pp. 8–19, on the limits upon such multiple meanings, which he expresses in the differences between fixed-associative logic, and mere free association.

23. David Stern, "Midrash and Indeterminacy," *Critical Inquiry* 15, no. 1 (Autumn 1988): 132–61; here quoting p. 155.

single text, without judgment as to which is closer to the "real" meaning, or without imposing "a hierarchy of meanings . . . like levels of interpretation that could in fact be ordered in an ascending ladder of significance."[24]

Later Jewish tradition, particularly the thirteenth-century writings of Moses de Leon in the Zohar and in Sefer Ha–Pardes and those of Baḥya ben Asher ibn Ḥalawa, did adopt such a hierarchical system of interpretation,[25] which fancifully refers to the study of the Bible as a walk through "paradise." The Hebrew term for paradise, pardes, is taken as an acronym for four hermeneutical approaches (Pᵊshat, Remez, Dᵊrash, Sod.)

The first approach is pᵊshat, the simplest literal meaning of a text: "You shall not murder" means just what it says, literally and with the full import of binding law.

A second hermeneutic is remez, an implicit hint, through numerology or acrostics, at further meanings in a biblical passage: "You shall not murder" numerologically equals 729; when added across (7 + 2 + 9), this equals 18, the equivalent of "life"; so life stems from refraining from murder, but one who commits murder may be subject to the death penalty.

The third approach is dᵊrash, homiletical exegesis based on linguistic patterns or rabbinic theology: "You shall not murder" may be explicated through a parable about a king's commands to his children not to steal his property, just as God commands that humanity not "steal" one another's souls, which are God's property.

Fourth and finally, rabbinic tradition considers biblical passages from the vantage point of sod, esoteric and mystical interpretations of biblical verses: "You shall not murder" not only commands humanity to respect the God-given gift of life, but also addresses the inner structure of the divine nature, bal-

---

24. Stern, "Midrash and Indeterminacy," p. 144.
25. See A. van der Heide, "PARDES: Methodological Reflections on the Theory of the Four Senses," in Journal of Jewish Studies 35, no. 2 (1983): 147–59.

ancing good and evil, power and quietude, masculine and feminine.[26]

It seems clear enough that such four-tiered systems of reading Scripture were intended not as a full summary of all medieval exegetical methods, but as "the programmatic expression of [the] conviction that the deepest meanings of Scripture are revealed in the teachings of the Kabbalah, teachings superceding all previous efforts."[27] At any rate, we may discern that traditional Judaic exegesis hardly approaches biblical texts in a monolithic manner, despite such depictions throughout Christian history.

The Spirit of the Law

What then of the spirit and theology that underlies the detailed performance of the bulk of Jewish law? Adherence to the rabbinic legal system has one principal goal: Jewish law serves as a straightforward guide toward a sanctified way of life.[28] Unlike Christianity's focus on redemption and salvation, a life guided by *halakhah*—the Jewish legal process—"consists of endless opportunities to sanctify the profane, opportunities to redeem the power of God from the chain of potentialities, opportunities to serve spiritual ends."[29] That simple fact, fun-

---

26. For a discussion of the many types of exegesis traditional to Judaism, see Moshe Greenberg, *Jewish Biblical Hermeneutics: Introductory Essays* (Hebrew) (Jerusalem: Bialik, 1983), pp. 60–67.
27. A. van der Heide, "PARDES," p. 149.
28. See Eliezer Berkovits, *Not in Heaven: On the Nature and Function of Halakhah* (New York: Ktav, 1983), p. 49, and Joseph B. Soloveitchik, *Halakhic Man* (Philadelphia, Pa.: Jewish Publication Society, 1983; originally published in Hebrew, 1944), pp. 19–29. Earlier, more apologetic versions of the claim that Judaism embodies true spirituality in its search for holiness can be found in Solomon Schechter, "The Law and Recent Criticism," in *Studies in Judaism*, 1st series (Philadelphia, Pa.: Jewish Publication Society, 1938), esp. pp. 233–51; see also Claude Goldsmid Montefiore, *Judaism and St. Paul: Two Essays* (New York: Arno Press, 1973; originally published, 1914), pp. 46–50, 92–94.
29. Abraham Joshua Heschel, *God in Search of Man: A Philosophy of Judaism* (New York: Farrar, Strauss and Giroux, 1955), p. 291.

damental for all Jewish law from the very inception of rabbinism, serves to explain Judaism's focus on detailed questions of law. There is a proper way to wash up in the morning, a special diet to eat, appropriate means to commemorate special occasions, a right way to farm God's holy earth. Each small detail of behavior expresses the larger message: the law, in specifying the proper modes of behavior for Jews, becomes *the* vehicle for morality and ethics, and more importantly, for holiness.[30]

Jewish legal literature also conveys rabbinic social policy. The law provides the foundations for institutions governing the family and education, as well as political and national consciousness. In the words of Jacob Neusner, it is "a grand design for the life of the house of Israel, the Jewish people, in all of its principal parts and requirements: time and space, both holy and profane, civil society and material economy, the cultic economy, making a secular living and shaping a holy life."[31] So in the details of law and obligation, the rabbis also captured their vision for the future of Israelite society, and imparted their worldview to all of later Judaism.

But the search for personal and communal holiness, found through living out the precepts of Torah, does not provide the full picture. As the rabbis developed the legal system, they also aimed to shape an individual's character through mental formation. Scholars of rabbinic literature agree that the quintessential rabbinic activity, study of the law (*Talmud Torah*), aims largely at teaching the student how to think.[32] Jewish law provides the casuistic framework and spells out possible choices in

---

30. See Jacob Neusner, "The Absoluteness of Christianity and the Uniqueness of Judaism," in *Interpretation: A Journal of Bible and Theology* 43, no. 1 (1989): 27–28.

31. Jacob Neusner, *Judaism: The Evidence of the Mishnah* (Chicago, Ill.: University of Chicago Press, 1981), p. ix.

32. See, for example, Jacob Neusner, *Invitation to the Talmud: A Teaching Book*, Rev. and expanded ed. (San Francisco, Calif.: Harper & Row, 1984), pp. 271–95. See also Adin Steinsaltz, *The Essential Talmud* (New York: Bantam Books, 1976; originally published in Hebrew), pp. 227–33; Steinsaltz makes a similar claim, although from a pastoral, not historical-critical, perspective.

each given situation. The student then is called upon to make, and rationally defend, an appropriate ruling.[33] This highlights the development of powers of abstraction from, and application to, particular cases. So Judasim—that is, Jewish law—is a thought process to be learned, and a set of principles and values to be inculcated.

Underlying Judaism's call for following the law, then, is a legal process based on a dialectic between thinking and disciplined observance. The law—the *halakhah*—is the center of the dialectical exchange. Disciplined attention, in thinking and practicing, to the entire process—not to some mere list of beliefs, no ortho-*doxy* here[34]—constitutes the spirit of the law. Jewish law's ability to tolerate and even foster dissent and independent thinking and rulings is rooted in this legal process. Even if one person or community skirts around the law as laid down by another, Judaism flourishes so long as the legal process remains intact. Or, to put it another way, God's desire is that Jews reflect upon and regulate their every action. But within the careful bounds of the halakhic system, God has imposed no arbitrary standard, even while laying forth an absolute and binding legal process.

---

33. In this realm of halakhic intellectual formation, one might reasonably follow Eugene B. Borowitz in arguing for Jewish individual autonomy (see "Autonomy and Its Limits," in *Reform Judaism Today*, vol. 3, *How We Live* [New York: Behrman House, 1978], pp. 45–55). Nonetheless, the Reform movement's (and Borowitz's) urging that Jews must "confront the claims of tradition" and then choose and create "new forms of Jewish life" falls somewhat short of capturing the entire halakhic process. Such a view fails to recognize fully the real limits upon creative autonomy imposed by adhering to and always orienting oneself toward an existing framework of case law and potential resolutions. For further discussion of the limits of the legal framework, see Jacob Neusner, "Talmudic Thinkingand Us," in *Invitation to the Talmud*, pp. 271–95, esp. pp. 277–79.

34. See Samuel C. Heilman, *Synagogue Life: A Study in Symbolic Interaction* (Chicago, Ill.: University of Chicago Press, 1973), pp. 5–18, for a similar observation.

A Judaic Approach to Legalism

Two recent works on rabbinic law (*halakhah*) help to clarify the nature of Jewish legalism. David Hartmann, in *A Living Covenant: The Innovative Spirit in Traditional Judaism*,[35] returns to the Moses-Sinai motif of earlier rabbinism and reinterprets the covenantal bond that links Jews to their God. He sees behind the *halakhah* a mutuality and complementarity between God's decrees and the human intellect. The legal impulse, in other words, can never be reduced to a mere fundamentalism; rather, the Jewish community itself must participate in laying forth the bounds of that legal commitment.

If covenantal mutuality is to be taken seriously, one's ethical and rational capacities must never be crushed. . . . In asking the Judaic community to interpret and expand the norms of Judaism to cover all aspects of life, the God of the covenant invites that community to trust its own ability to make rational and moral judgments.[36]

So it is that the goal of participation in the system of law need not be limited to mere formal or knee-jerk regulation of daily activity. On the contrary, the regulation of each and every act is the basis for confronting the existential quandaries that plague humanity and that find expression in such questions as "What is the meaning of life?" or "How can we explain the existence of good and evil?"

The significance Jews find in their way of life and the compelling spiritual power of the Torah can act as a counterbalance to despair, enabling us to live by the covenant despite the pain of tragedy. Our covenantal anthropology thus allows an individual to satisfy the passion for theism within partial frameworks of intelligibility, to hope without the certainty of redemption.[37]

---

35. See note 3, above.
36. Hartmann, *A Living Covenant*, pp. 97–98.
37. Hartmann, *A Living Covenant*, p. 277.

It follows that Jewish convenantal anthropology—and theology, I might add—does not imply a lifeless pursuit of juridical trivia. The point is rather a process, encompassing both a legally oriented behavior and a legally oriented intellectual program, that directs the Jew to a sanctified life. Through the "life of Torah," Jews derive meaning and orientation, even while recognizing the vitality of discrete laws.[38]

Eliezer Berkovits, a leading progressive interpreter of Jewish legal theory today, addresses similar problems of the purported inflexibility of Jewish law in *Not in Heaven: On the Nature and Function of Halakhah.*[39] Berkovits places heavy emphasis on the role of ethical and pragmatic impulses in determining how a law actually might be put into effect.[40]

The affairs of men cannot be guided by absolute objectivity, but only by human subjectivity. What God desires of the Jewish people is that it live by [God's] Word in accordance with its own understanding. . . . When it is necessary to make decisions for human conduct and behavior, one can do so only on the basis of . . . pragmatic principles; for example, "Follow the view of the majority." The result is not objective truth but pragmatic validity.[41]

Berkovitz's use of the essentially modern terms "subjectivity" and "pragmatic" helps to explain, in part, the role of humanity in the halakhic process. Yet in light of the rabbis' contention that God's decrees underlie and provide the authority for rules derived through halakhic means, we need not follow him in asserting that human participation in the legal process reduces

---

38. The same broad perspective is taken in David Novak, *Halakhah in a Theological Dimension,* Brown Judaic Studies 68 (Chico, Calif.: Scholars Press, 1985), pp. 1–10, where the emphasis in on the authoritative, yet changeable nature of *halakhah.*
39. See note 28, above.
40. A classic formulation of the relationship between ethics and *halakhah* is found in Aharon Lichtenstein, "Does Jewish Tradition Recognize an Ethic Independent of *Halakhah?*" in Menachem Marc Kellner, ed., *Contemporary Jewish Ethics* (New York: Sanhedrin Press, 1978), pp. 102–23.
41. Berkovits, *Not in Heaven,* p. 49.

that process to subjectivity. Still, given the central role Berkovitz accords to the subjective human element in the acceptance of the Torah, we can easily understand his concern for the integrity of the halakhic process. Jewish leaders may determine—humanly, subjectively, or better, through their endorsement of and participation in *halakhah*—that a particular action, ordinarily permitted by the law, is to be avoided. But Berkovitz urges no willy-nilly supersession of the law, but rather a careful and considered invocation of halakhic principles.

A superficial study may give the impression that often, instead of outrightly rejecting a biblical command, the *Halakhah* attempts to get around it.[42]

The coordination [between the revealed Word of God and the human world] is possible because the word of man in this case is a disciple of the revealed one. The teachers of Israel are people who are committed to the Torah from Sinai, who heard the Voice, who are absorbed in the tradition of Israel's effort through the ages to render the bequest of the Tablets life-guarding and life-forming. When they then speak their word in accordance with their understanding, they indeed teach one of the "forty-nine faces" of the Torah given to man on Sinai.[43]

The law thus allows for the alteration of human action only in the context of a legal process that it never seeks to nullify.

Three impulses emerge in this legal application, namely, the integrity of the legal system, the original intent of a given rule, and straightforward practicality. Let me briefly provide an example for each of these principles as it might be applied in a critique of a particular halakhic case.

The Integrity of the Law: Absolution of Vows and Oaths

Taking a vow or oath that invoked God's name was considered a very serious matter in ancient Israel. Misuse of God's name would constitute a direct violation of the Third Com-

---

42. Berkovits, *Not in Heaven*, p. 75.
43. Berkovits, *Not in Heaven*, pp. 81–82.

mandment. Biblical sources are quite explicit in this regard: rash oaths were discouraged, and all were urged to fulfill their vows with quick dispatch (cf. Deut. 23:21–23, or the disastrous effects of Jepthah's foolish vow to sacrifice the first thing to emerge from his house if God gave him victory in battle, Judg. 4:30–40).

Clearly, however, sometimes people made promises or vows they could not or never fully intended to keep. Taking note of this fact, the rabbis of the early centuries of the Common Era developed procedures whereby such vows might be absolved, rather than allowed to go utterly neglected.[44] Their goal was to prevent biblical law's careful strictures against using God's name needlessly from becoming moribund. Yet these authorities maintained that the legal process must remain in force, even if through it we allow actions or refuse to recognize words and deeds that otherwise would have serious legal effect. In short, this example demonstrates that, in order to protect the legal system as a whole, the rabbis allowed for flexibility, even while maintaining the integrity of legal strictures.

The Intent of the Law: The Writ of Noncancelable Debt (Prozbul)

Biblical law provides that every seven years all debts between Israelites are to be canceled (Deut. 15:1–3).[45] The original purpose of this debt cancelation was to assure fair and equitable flow of money throughout the entire Israelite community—no family would become overly enriched, none too economically deprived, because every seven years debts were released and every fifty years all real estate returned to its original family owners. Money and land were to be lent, not actually passed in perpetuity.

---

44. See Jacob Neusner, *A History of the Mishnaic Law of Women* (Leiden: E.J. Brill, 1980), part 3, pp. 3–8; part 5, pp. 107–24.
45. For a study of this injunction and its legacy in rabbinic law, see Louis E. Newman, *The Sanctity of the Seventh Year: A Study of Mishnah Tractate Shebiit*, Brown Judaic Studies 44 (Chico, Calif.: Scholars Press, 1983), esp. pp. 16–17, 29, and 199–213.

Rabbinic literature records that a problem arose in this regard. Those who had money did not wish to lend it to poor people within a year or two of the Sabbatical, lest the money not be repaid on time and the loan thus canceled outright. The rabbinic authorities, taking this practice and the original intent of the law into account, developed a procedure whereby a creditor might symbolically transfer privately held debts to a court (through a transfer writ called a *prozbul*), which then could enforce collection even during the Sabbatical year. The result was a return to the regular flow of money throughout the entire community, without fear that deadbeats might abuse the system. Here the rabbis utilized a legal means to preserve the original intent of a biblical enactment.

The Practicality of the Law: The Sale of Leaven during Passover.

My third and final example moves from the integrity of the law and its original intent to a matter of its practical application. Biblical regulations specify that during Passover each Israelite must utterly remove any trace of leaven from the home and from all ownership: one is forbidden to eat, touch, possess, or even to own any leavened product or any leavening agent (see, for example, Exod. 13:3–8).

For their part, the rabbis slowly extended the ban not just to foodstuffs, but to all utensils ever used in preparation of such food.[46] In all, this amounted to a total ban on most ordinary foods and certainly on all normal food preparation techniques and establishments. How then might the Israelite community comply with the ban? In order to address this practical problem, the rabbis again found in the law a means to address the problem: while forbidden to own or personally possess leaven, Jews were permitted to store such items in their homes if the leaven-tainted items belonged to a gentile. So the rabbis advo-

---

46. See Baruch M. Bokser, *The Origins of the Seder: The Passover Rite and Early Rabbinic Judaism* (Berkeley: University of California Press, 1984), esp. pp. 20, 76–100.

cated selling all leavened products and utensils to a gentile for a sum of money, and then repurchasing the food and dishes eight days later, after Passover. This legal act aimed at allowing the law to continue to grow and encompass further areas of life in a practicable way. Proof of that practicability to our own day is found in thousands of Jewish communities across the world who participate each year in this legal process.

The spirit of biblical revelation, as the rabbis saw matters, resided in the constant application of legal procedure, not in the particular ruling or outcome in a given instance. Judaism, in the rabbinic era and beyond, was not a religion of wooden legalism, but of soaring intellect, of humane and studied adherence to an overarching set of principles for daily conduct, found in the Torah. Once again in the words of Eliezer Berkovitz:

> The Torah was given to the people of Israel. It obligates the Jew to study it and to seek to understand it; it demands of the sages of Israel that they interpret it and teach it as guidance and law for everyday living. . . . Whatever is discovered in it by human beings who accept the Torah as God's revelation to the Jewish people at Sinai and study it is indeed the truth of the Torah. . . . [47]

So it is that, based on their own reading of contemporaneous culture, the earliest rabbinic legislators worked with and developed Scripture's priorities. Biblical material in general, and the Ten Commandments in particular, provided a guide to legal options, such that Sinaitic revelation was the foundation for human involvement in the legal enterprise. The rabbinic promotion of innovation and flexibility, and the case-by-case approach to the law it engenders, promised a dynamic process. Filtered through the rabbinic consistory, particular conditions and changing times combined with the received tradition, and the regulations thus put forth in turn would become the core

---

47. Berkovits, *Not in Heaven*, p. 51.

of the next generation's received law. As we shall see in the upcoming chapters, rabbinic regulations involving the Decalogue thus were constantly adjusted and readjusted, ever new and always fresh, continually maintaining adherence to the Sinaitic revelation.

2. The Ten Commandments within Nascent Judaism

Within the Bible itself, the Ten Commandments have a special status, expressing God's direct speech to the Israelites gathered at Mount Sinai (see Exod. 20:1 and Deut. 5:4–5). But if the rabbinic treatment of the Decalogue is to exemplify the Judaic approach to all biblical materials, we require more context. For, as we shall see, in the rabbinic mind, the Ten Commandments were but one part of a larger movement to return to Sinai, while confronting at the same time a rapidly changing world.

The Centerpiece of Biblical Law: The Ten Utterances

The narrative of Moses' ascent to Sinai tells one of the most moving stories in all of the Pentateuchal materials. From Moses' lowly origins to royal bearing, and from Egypt to the Land of Israel and back again, the episodes captivate both popular and scholarly literature.

The narrative as found in Exodus consists of six parts:

1. Moses' birth and youth as a slave in Egypt (Exod. 1:1–2:14);
2. his life in the Sinai desert with his father-in-law, Jethro, and his wife, Zipporah (Exod. 2:15–2:25);
3. his first encounter with God on Mount Sinai and his subsequent challenge to Pharaoh through the ten plagues (Exod. 3:1–12:32);
4. the Israelites' flight from Egyptian captivity to the Red Sea and to the Sinai wilderness (Exod. 12:33–18:27);

5. Moses' ascent to Sinai, the revelation of the Ten Commandments, Covenant Code, and the plans for the Tabernacle (Exod. 19:1–31:18);
6. the Israelites' submission to and redemption from the slavery of idolatry as they worshipped a golden calf (Exod. 32:1–35).

The manner in which this Pentateuchal story is arranged and passed on expresses a strong bias against idolatrous activity of any kind. Three concentric frames have been arranged so as to encompass these events. First, the entire story is bracketed by two accounts of the Israelites' slavery, first to the Egyptian man-god, Pharaoh, and at the end to the idolatrous worship of a man-made god, the golden calf. Second, and internal to these recurring episodes of slavery, the narrative is further balanced by Moses' two meetings with God on Mount Sinai, one before and one after the Israelites' exodus. Finally, the middle of the story depicts Moses' return to Egypt as an adult and his departure as the leader of the Israelite nation.

Slavery and Redemption	God's Appearances	To Egypt and Back
1. Slavery to Pharaoh	2. Sinai with Jethro: God's Appearance	3. Moses vs. Pharaoh
6. Slavery to Idolatry	5. Sinai with Israel: God's Revelation	4. Exodus from Egypt

Each part of this drama adds to the narrative tension, but I would argue that the penultimate act, the Sinaitic revelation of the Ten Commandments (Act 5), stands out as the literary focal point. God's revelation caps the entire Egyptian portion of the saga, creates the bridge between the exodus and all that follows, and provides the legislative foil for the upcoming incident regarding the golden calf.[1]

So the revelation on Sinai represents one crucial episode in the saga, if not the turning point of the whole. That legal revelation itself, however, has one paramount component. During the theophany at Sinai, a myriad of rules were transmitted to Moses, yet only the Ten Commandments were immediately chiseled in stone for posterity. It would be more than fair to assert that the Ten Commandments encapsulate the whole Pentateuchal theophany. Even within the Bible itself, they are paradigmatic of God's legislation and directives for the people of Israel (see, for example, Exod. 34:28). Judaism, in referring to these basic and fundamental rules, has always highlighted the special nature of their revelation by referring to them as "the Ten Utterances" (ʿaseret ha-dibbrot), the ten quintessential statements of God to the Israelite nation.

Two apparently contradictory themes characterize the rabbinic treatment of the Ten Utterances, exemplified here in discussions of Jewish liturgical practice. One follows the lead of the Hebrew Bible's narrative, according the Ten Utterances absolute centrality within Jewish prayer. The other impulse, as we shall see, is to downplay the role of the Sinaitic commandments within the liturgy, so as to emphasize the full revelation to Moses, including far more material than just these ten rules.

To show first the prominence of the Ten Utterances, let us turn to a Talmudic discourse on the daily liturgy, one major portion of which proclaims God's monotheistic character and special relationship to the Jewish people. This prayer, called the *Shema*, actually is composed of three scriptural passages:

---

1. See Levenson, *Sinai and Zion*, pp. 42–45, for the claim that the Ten Commandments are primary to this narrative, not on literary grounds but based on a theology of *miṣvah* (command). A similar statement recognizing the character of the Israelite covenant is found in Nahum M. Sarna, *Exploring Exodus: The Heritage of Biblical Israel* (New York: Schocken Books, 1986), pp. 110–11. See also Brevard S. Childs, *Introduction to the Old Testament as Scripture* (Philadelphia, Pa.: Fortress Press, 1979), pp. 165–74.

Deuteronomy 6:4–9

Hear, O Israel! The LORD is our God, the LORD alone. You shall love the LORD your God with all your heart and with all your soul and with all your might. Take to heart these instructions with which I charge you this day. Impress them upon your children. Recite them when you stay at home and when you are away, when you lie down and when you get up. Bind them as a sign on your hand and let them serve as a symbol on your forehead; inscribe them on the doorposts of your house and on your gates.

Deuteronomy 11:13–21

If, then, you obey the commandments that I enjoin upon you this day, loving the LORD your God and serving [God] with all your heart and soul, I will grant the rain for your land in season, the early rain and the late. You shall gather in your new grain and wine and oil—I will also provide grass in the fields for your cattle—and thus you shall eat your fill. Take care not to be lured away to serve other gods and bow down to them. For the LORD's anger will flare up against you, and [the LORD] will shut up the skies so that there will be no rain and the ground will not yield its produce; and you will soon perish from the good land that the LORD is assigning to you.

Therefore impress these My words upon your very heart: bind them as a sign on your hand and let them serve as a symbol on your forehead, and teach them to your children—reciting them when you stay at home and when you are away, when you lie down and when you get up; and inscribe them on the doorposts of your house and on your gates—to the end that you and your children may endure, in the land that the LORD swore to your fathers to assign to them, as long as there is a heaven over the earth.

Numbers 15:37–41

The LORD said to Moses as follows: Speak to the Israelite people and instruct them to make for themselves fringes on the corners of their garments throughout the ages; let them attach a cord of blue to the fringe at each corner. That shall be your fringe; look at it and recall all the commandments of the LORD and observe them, so that you do not follow your heart and eyes in your lustful urge. Thus you shall be reminded to observe all My commandments and to be holy to your God. I the LORD am your God, who brought you out of the land of Egypt to be your God; I, the LORD your God.

According to rabbinic law, the *Shema's* concatenation of verses must be recited twice daily, once each morning, once each evening. Yet the rabbis are not in agreement on the reason for this mandatory, twice-daily recitation. In reviewing this talmudic argument, we shall see the first clear interpretive trend, which accords a prominent place to the Ten Utterances.

Yerushalmi Berakhot 1:5 [Venice: 3c; Vilna: 9a–b]

Why should Jews recite the portions [that make up the *Shema*] two [times] each and every day?

R. Levi and R. Simon [had the following dispute]:

R. Simon said, "[Jews should recite these passages twice daily] because concerning [the *Shema* Scripture] states both [the time of] laying down and rising up. [Since Deut. 6:7 lists two times, the *Shema* ought to be recited evening and morning.]

R. Levi said, "[Jews should recite the *Shema* two times daily] because the Ten Utterances are contained within them:

"(1) '*I the* LORD *am your God* . . . ' (Exod. 20:2a)—[corresponds to] '*Hear, O Israel! The* LORD *is our God* . . . ' (Deut. 6:4a).

"(2) '*You shall have no other gods besides Me*' (Exod. 20:3)—[corresponds to] ' *. . . the* LORD *alone*' (Deut. 6:4b).

"(3) '*You shall not swear falsely by the name of the* LORD *your God*' (Exod. 20:7a)—[corresponds to] '*You shall love the* LORD *your God* . . . ' (Deut. 6:5a), for one who truly loves the King could not swear falsely using his name.

"(4) '*Remember the Sabbath day and keep it holy*' (Exod. 20:8)—[corresponds to] '*Thus you shall be reminded [to observe all My commandments]* . . . ' (Num. 15:40a). Rabbi says, 'This commandment of Sabbath is equal in weight to all other commandments in the Torah, for [concerning the Sabbath], it is written [in Scripture], "You made known to them Your holy Sabbath, and You ordained for them laws, commandments, and teaching . . . " (Neh. 9:14a). [The verse's reference to Sabbath is intended] to inform you that it is equal in weight to all other commandments of the Torah.'

"(5) *'Honor your father and your mother . . . '* (Exod. 20:12a)—[corresponds to] *' . . . to the end that you and your children may endure . . . '* (Deut. 11:21a).

"(6) *'You shall not murder'* (Exod. 20:13a)—[corresponds to] *'and you will soon perish [from the good land that the* Lord *is assigning to you]'* (Deut. 11:17b), for anyone who murders will be murdered.

"(7) *'You shall not commit adultery'* (Exod. 20:13b)—[corresponds to] *' . . . so that you do not follow your heart and eyes in your lustful urge'* (Num. 15:39b). Said R. Levi, 'Heart and eyes are two agents of transgression, for [concerning them] it is written [in Scripture], "*Give your heart to me, my son; let your eyes watch my ways*" (Prov. 23:26). [That is to say], the Holy, Blessed One said, "If you give Me your heart and eyes, then alone shall I know that you are with Me."'

"(8) *'You shall not steal'* (Exod. 20:13c)—[corresponds to] *'You shall gather in your new grain . . . '* (Deut. 11:14b), but not your neighbor's grain.

"(9) *'You shall not not bear false witness against your neighbor,'* for I the Lord am your God (Exod. 20:13d)—[corresponds to] that which is written [as a nonscriptural conclusion to the *Shema* passage], 'The Lord your God is true.' What is the meaning of 'true?' Said R. Avun, '[This means that the Lord] is the living God and the eternal king.' Said R. Levi, 'The Holy, Blessed One said, "If you offer false testimony against your fellow, I shall consider that transgression as if you had offered false testimony against Me, to the effect that I did not create the heavens and the earth."'

"(10) *'You shall not covet your neighbor's house'* (Exod. 20:14a)—[corresponds to] *'Inscribe them on the doorposts of your house'* (Deut. 6:9a): your house, but not your neighbor's house."

In R. Levi's opinion, each word or phrase in the *Shema* prayer corresponds directly to one of the Ten Commandments. So recitation of that prayer was considered tantamount to reading and studying the Ten Utterances themselves. But, given his opinion, why recite the *Shema* twice daily (the question that prompted this entire passage)? The answer is implicit, supplied by the surrounding context in the Talmud. The first recitation of the *Shema*, in the morning, is to be taken at face value: each Jew proclaims the absolute monotheism of God, and restates the fundamentals of the covenant that binds the Jewish people to God alone. The evening recitation of the *Shema*, however, fulfills a separate duty incumbent upon all Jews, namely, remembrance of the exodus from Egypt during the evening prayers. The worshipper does this by reciting scriptural passages— the *Shema*—reminiscent of the Ten Commandments and the entire Sinaitic cycle.

As we have seen, this tightly and carefully constructed Talmudic passage elegantly connects two great literary pieces of Jewish prayer. But it further indicates a theological position that reveals a paramount rabbinic conviction: the Ten Utterances are quintessential to Judaism. They are as basic and foundational as the simple assertion that there is but one God. The rabbis, in short, were careful and attentive interpreters of Scripture and its injunctions. Just as the Ten Commandments stood as the highlight of God's Sinaitic revelation, and as the pinnacle of the entire story of the Israelites in Egypt, so rabbinic literature placed these laws at the heart of all Judaism.

I indicated above, however, that a second—and seemingly altogether different—attitude characterizes rabbinic thought regarding the Ten Utterances. In this viewpoint, the foundational Ten Utterances are moved painstakingly out of the center of rabbinic theology, made only as important as any other piece of the scriptural legacy. This passage (which immediately follows the dispute between Rabbi Simon and Rabbi Levi) opens by once again equating the *Shema* and the Ten Commandments, but then quickly moves on to soften the prominence of the Sinaitic commands.

Yerushalmi Berakhot 1:5 [Venice: 3c; Vilna: 9b]

In a separate context we teach: [During the daily offering], the overseer told them, "Pronounce a blessing," and they did so (M. Tamid 5:1A).

What was the substance of the blessing? R. Matenah said in the name of Samuel, "This was the Blessing for Torah."

And they read the Ten Commandments, followed by [the three paragraphs of] the Shema, [including "Hear, O Israel" (Deut. 6:4–9)], the passage be-

ginning, "Now if you hearken . . . " (Deut. 11:13–21), and the passage beginning, "The LORD spoke to Moses . . . " (Num. 15:37–41) (M. Tamid 5:1B).

R. Ami in the name of Resh Laqish, "This proves that the blessings [before and after the *Shema,* which are not mentioned,] are dispensable."

Said R. Ba, "Nothing! You may infer nothing from this! For the Ten Utterances, [which were recited together with the *Shema*], constitute the very essence of the *Shema* [and so replace its blessings].

For Rav Matenah and R. Samuel bar Nahman both said, "In accord with strict logic, people should recite the Ten Utterances every day. So why shouldn't people recite them? Because of arguments advanced by heretics to the effect that the Ten Commandments alone were given to Moses on Sinai."[2]

The rabbis here strike a crucial balance. While they recognize that the Ten Commandments ought to have a prominent role in worship, they nonetheless recognize that people must omit them altogether, and for good reason. Rabbinic theology embraces the notion that God revealed the entire Pentateuch for Moses to record upon Mount Sinai. Each and every part of the written Scripture equally represents God's eternal law, God's Torah. The written law, Judaism holds, was accompanied by oral supplementary and complementary rules (later codified in the Mishnah). This belief in the integrity of the Dual Torah[3]— both written and oral—is the reason for the exclusion of the Ten Commandments from daily worship rites. If a single portion of the Torah were to be recited—especially a passage so central to the narrative of the Sinaitic theophany—people might be led to believe falsely that only that passage, the Ten Commandments,

---

2. For parallel passages, see B. Berakhot 11b–12b and B. Tamid 35a.
3. For a statement of Judaic theology of the Dual Torah, see Fred Rosner, *Moses Maimonides' Commentary on the Mishnah: Introduction to Seder Zeraim and Commentary on Tractate Berakhot,* English translation with notes and general introduction (New York: Feldheim Publishers, 1975), pp. 65–67, 74–81. A modern theological counterpart is found in Jacob Neusner, *The Enchantments of Judaism: Rites of Transformation from Birth through Death* (New York: Basic Books, 1987), pp. 17–28, 167–93.

in fact was revealed at Mount Sinai, that the remainder was a later creation of lesser authority. The incisive rabbinic legislation prevents this type of exclusive importance being attached to the Ten Commandments.

Rabbinic literature, then, allows an apparent contradiction in its opinion to stand. The Ten Utterances represent the heart of all Judaic theology. But, they are no more important than any other bit of the revealed law of Judaism.

Such an ambivalence regarding the Ten Utterances is reflected also in modern synagogue practice: during the yearly course of reciting the entire Pentateuch in weekly portions, the congregation reads an account of the Sinaitic revelation two times (one version found in Exod. 20; a second in Deut. 5). Some congregations have the custom of standing while these portions of the Torah scroll are read, in order to demonstrate the importance of the Ten Utterances and to symbolically stand together with the Israelites at the base of Mount Sinai. Yet just as many congregations follow the opposite practice, and remain seated during the proclamation. This posture indicates that no single portion of the Pentateuch is any more crucial or essential than any other. The Ten Commandments simply are one more part— but only on equal footing with all others—of the Sinaitic revelation. To stand at this juncture alone would be to denigrate all the remainder of the Pentateuch.[4]

Defining the Judaic Context: From the Mishnah to the Talmud of the Land of Israel

The core of Judaic theology, including rabbinic attitudes toward the Ten Utterances, assumed the written form which we now possess in a literary flourish that spanned nearly six cen-

---

4. On the Torah service, see Joseph H. Hertz, *The Authorized Daily Prayer Book: Hebrew Text, English Translation, with Commentary and Notes*. Rev. ed. (New York: Bloch Publishers, 1985; originally published 1948), pp. 470–95.

turies at the beginning of the Common Era. Materials put in writing during those early years of the rabbinic movement constitute the legacy of—and our principal evidence for—the emerging Jewish consensus on the content and substance of the oral portions of the law transmitted throughout the centuries. The rabbinic legislators in the Land of Israel compiled their rulings into a law book, called the Mishnah (ca. 200 c.e.). The Mishnah set the tone for all later Judaic legal development, and most nonlegal literature as well.

The Mishnah's text reflects the rabbinic approach (both linguistically and substantively) toward its biblical antecedents, as the rabbis developed a set of extended essays on critical topics (for example, the nature of sacred time and space), so as to argue in behalf of the rabbinic worldview. These various topics constituted a theological network representing three major interests: *priestly* attention to holiness, *scribal* concerns for the correspondence of word and act, and ordinary *householders'* regard for daily conduct.[5]

The theological program of the Mishnah expresses the rabbinic mind,[6] which was neither fundamentalistic nor solely determined by legislative needs. Instead, the Mishnah often read the Hebrew Bible in quite unpredictable ways, at times seeming to ignore basic scriptural strictures. For example, biblical materials ruled that anything placed upon the altar immediately became

---

5. See Neusner, *Judaism: The Evidence of the Mishnah*, pp. 122–26.
6. In referring to "the rabbinic mind," or "the rabbinic movement," I of course do not mean to obscure the clear differences in emphasis and interest expressed in various rabbinic texts: the Mishnah, for example, has its clear interests in propounding and preserving the status quo, while Genesis and Leviticus Rabbah form judgments upon the meaning of Israel's history. Rather, throughout the volume I use such terms to point toward the larger whole to which the evidence of the Talmud of the Land of Israel—the document principally under study here—attests, a "system of Judaism . . . [expressed in] at least eleven compilations of biblical exegesis, the Tosefta, the entirety of the Babylonian Talmud, and various other minor tractates, compositions of prayers, and other writings of rabbis in late antiquity" (Jacob Neusner, *Judaism in Society: The Evidence of the Yerushalmi: Toward the Natural History of a Religion* [Chicago, Ill.: University of Chicago Press, 1983], p. 116).

sanctified, *ex opere operato* (for example, see Exod. 29:37). As the Mishnah developed such precepts, it held that consecrated status could be conferred only with the priest's proper intention.[7] This development fits within the Mishnah's overall concern with the relationship between a person's actions and intention. In like fashion throughout the Mishnah, the major ideas expressed are built upon, but not limited to, a solid understanding of the scriptural account, as handed down by the rabbis. So, too, the Mishnah's interests did not reflect real legislative settings alone. The overwhelming bulk of the Mishnaic law addressed the Temple and its regular maintenance, a full 130 years after the Temple had been destroyed.

Even years after the Temple's destruction, the rabbis' clear aim in compiling the Mishnah was to establish continuity in Jewish life. The Temple as an institution and its rites were to continue as the center of Judaic theology, thus demanding both personal and national purity and sanctity. The requirement of holiness, expressed throughout the Mishnah, stems from the particularity of God's relationship with Israel. What must a Jew do to reflect the special relationship between self and God? How does one cooperate in God's overall scheme? The six major divisions that comprise the Mishnah addressed the relationship between God, Israel, and sanctification through exacting, detailed inquiry.

I. *The division of agriculture:* How does God's ownership of the Land of Israel affect Israelites' use of that Land and its produce?

II. *The division of appointed times:* How does God's interaction with Israel in history serve to orient the calendar, marking out special times requiring special actions by Israelites?

---

7. See Howard Eilberg-Schwartz, *The Human Will in Judaism: The Mishnah's Philosophy of Intention,* Brown Judaic Studies 103 (Atlanta, Ga.: Scholars Press, 1986), 149–63.

III. *The division of women:* How does the special sanctity demanded of Israelites by God affect their relationships within the family unit, and especially with women?

IV. *The division of damages:* How does the unity and equality of God's holy people Israel demand special action in business, government, and day-to-day dealings?

V. *The division of holy things:* How does the worship of God demand special action in the Temple, God's holy locus?

VI. *The division of purities:* How does extending the holiness required in God's Temple to everyday life demand special attention to all aspects of life vis-à-vis cultic purity?

Central to understanding the Mishnah's importance as the focal point of Jewish life are the basic assumptions of the system as a whole and in each of its parts, which I summarize as follows:

God owns the Holy Land [Division of Agriculture], and gives it to the people with whom he has had a long-standing historical relationship [Division of Appointed Times], namely Israel (hence the appropriate Judaic idiom, the Land of Israel). The Israelites owe God and his appointed representatives payment for their use of the Land [Divisions of Agriculture and Holy Things], in addition to special actions in response to God's dealings with them in history [Division of Appointed Times]. The holiness required in God's worship must also inform mundane activity [Division of Purities], extending to both levels of the Israelite clan—one's own immediate family [Division of Women] and the larger family of the Children of Israel [Division of Damages].

The early rabbinic intellectual and theological system, embedded in the details of the Mishnah's rules, provided the forum for the continuance between the revelation at Sinai and later rabbinic thought. It was complemented by other works, notably the Tosefta (a similar supplement compiled one generation later), as well as midrashic literature, much of which aims at connecting the legal traditions explicitly with the Hebrew Bible and its concerns. In even closer fashion, the Mishnah provided the

starting point for the two Talmuds, which at least formally
constitute paragraph-by-paragraph commentaries upon it.[8]
The theological program of the Mishnah, as well as its basic
categories of law and thought, have endured throughout, and
in fact continue to define, the rabbinic movement.

It follows, therefore, that the Mishnah is the first step in examining rabbinic attitudes toward the Ten Commandments.
Several matters stand out clearly, constituting scant evidence of
early interest within the rabbinic movement of the Land of Israel.

First, the Ten Utterances are mentioned only two times in the
entire Mishnah, some 1,137 pages in the most recent English
translation.[9] One of these passages, analyzed above, discusses
the recitation of the Ten Utterances in the daily liturgy (Mishnah Tamid 5:1). The other, an equally brief and fleeting reference, determines the day of the year on which Moses shattered
the stone tablets, marking that as a fast day (Mishnah Taanit
4:6, further analyzed below in chapter 4 of this volume). In
other words, the Sinaitic revelation as an event plays a rather
minimal role in the discussions found in the Mishnah's law.

Second, the Mishnah's organization moved away from the
content of the Ten Commandments. Only three of the Commandments are represented in the Mishnah by tractate-length
essays: (1) The injunction in Exodus 20:3–5, "You shall have no
other gods besides Me. . . . You shall not bow down to them
or serve them," in some measure gives rise to a tractate on
avoidance of contact with idolators, *Avodah Zarah* (Foreign Worship). (2) The rule found at Exodus 20:7, "You shall not swear
falsely by the name of the LORD your God," more or less pre-

---

8. Introductory essays on the rabbinic canon may be found in Jacob Neusner,
   Invitation to the Talmud; and *Invitation to Midrash: A Teaching Book: The Workings
   of Rabbinic Bible Interpretation* (San Francisco, Calif.: Harper & Row, 1989). See
   also Hermann L. Strack, *Einleitung in Talmud und Midrasch,* Revised and Edited by Günter Stemberger (Munich: C. H. Beck, 1982).
9. Jacob Neusner, *The Mishnah: A New Translation* (New Haven, Conn.: Yale
   University Press, 1988).

sages the materials found in tractates *Shevuot* (Oaths) and *Nedarim* (Vows), although other biblical materials, Leviticus 5:1–3 and Numbers 30:2–16, better correspond to the Mishnah's interests here in family law and the cultic implications of rash oaths. (3) The simple command Exodus 20:8 to "Remember the Sabbath day and keep it holy" is reflected in a far-reaching tractate devoted to defining the public and private domain for Sabbath law, *Shabbat* (the Sabbath).

Ten Commandments	Mishnaic Tractates
1. The LORD is Israel's God	
2. Other gods forbidden	Avodah Zarah
3. Vain use of God's name forbidden	Shevuot and Nedarim
4. Sanctify the Sabbath	Shabbat
5. Honor of parents	
6. Murder forbidden	
7. Adultery forbidden	
8. Theft forbidden	
9. False Testimony forbidden	
10. Covetousness forbidden	

These three cases highlight the degree to which the Mishnah studiously avoided the Ten Commandments as an organizing principle. Only four of sixty-three tractates fully devote themselves to individual Commandments, and this attention is largely topical, not exegetical or principally aimed at these verses in particular. Only three individual Commandments come directly under the pen of the Mishnaic authors, and even here the rabbis adopt largely their own agenda. Furthermore, not a single Mishnaic tractate is devoted to the history or miraculous character of the Sinaitic revelation.

Of course, the Mishnah *does* contain material relevant to some, even all, of the other Commandments, scattered here and there throughout its outline and framework. Early rabbinic materials regarding murder, for example, are found in the three

Neziqin tractates and in tractate *Sanhedrin.* Yet in these discussions, the Mishnah merely assumes, but rarely invokes, the command "You shall not murder" (Exod. 20:13; Deut. 5:17). Instead, the substance of the discussion concerns the delineation of premeditated murder as opposed to accidental killing or manslaughter. So, in discussing murder, the Mishnah focuses not on the Sixth Commandment per se, but on other biblical passages that afford such a distinction (Exod. 21:12–13; Num. 35:16–23: Deut. 19:4–11).

The crucial point to observe is that the rabbis who edited the Mishnah and set the agenda for later legal work apparently had no intention to analyze the Ten Commandments in any systematic fashion.[10] No redactional pattern corresponds to these rules; many are dealt with only in quite different biblical contexts. Given the larger goal of the rabbinic legislators, the Mishnah's silence in regard to the Ten Utterances need not surprise us. The religious return to Sinai urged by the rabbis, after all, can be realized only when their halakhic process points the way.

In light of the Mishnah's relative silence, however, later rabbinic compositions likewise do not afford us well-organized essays on each of the Utterances. Rather, as we turn to the first rabbinic legal document that has a sizeable amount of material regarding the Ten Commandments, namely, the Talmud of the Land of Israel, we must consider many individual passages, each taken out of its Talmudic setting. These discourses will illumine the early rabbinic attitude toward the Ten Utterances, and also exemplify the rabbinic theology of Scripture.

The Talmud of the Land of Israel (also, Jerusalem Talmud or Talmud Yerushalmi), a compilation of third through fifth-century legal thought, formed in Tiberias, Caesarea, Sepphoris,

---

10. By contrast, see midrashic treatments, especially those of Mekhilta de-Rabbi Ishmael and Pesikhta de-Rav Kahana, which I discuss in chapter 3 of this volume.

and Lydda, for the most part undertakes to explain and clarify the Mishnah. Most characteristic of the Talmud are passages that pay careful attention to the underlying Mishnaic materials. Some cite, gloss, or amplify the exact language of the Mishnaic phrase, while others juxtapose and harmonize two independent Mishnaic passages. A second major thrust in the Talmud of the Land of Israel is its relatively independent analysis of the Mishnah's legal principles. Here we find units that expand and amplify the law either by citing relevant passages from the Tosefta or through fresh, "Talmudic" inquiry, citations of illustrative cases, whether concrete or hypothetical, and prooftexts adduced from the Hebrew Bible for the Mishnaic law under consideration.[11] Within this range of interest in aspects of the Mishnah, we will find revealed as well entirely unprecedented modes of inquiry developed in the two centuries from the closure of the Mishnah to the redaction of the Talmud.

In fact, the Talmud of the Land of Israel comprises our best literary evidence for the development of Judaic legal thought within Israel in the period after the Mishnah's closure.[12] Yet this document has gone largely unstudied, even ignored by historians of religion and law.[13] This is for two reasons, one having

---

11. See Jacob Neusner, *The Talmud of the Land of Israel: A Preliminary Translation and Explanation*, Vol. 35, *Introduction: Taxonomy* (Chicago, Ill.: University of Chicago Press, 1983), p. 96.
12. In this study, I am concerned with the depiction and usage of the Ten Commandments within the Talmud of the Land of Israel, embracing the documentary approach undergirded by the theoretical advances of Jacob Neusner. The Babylonian Talmud does, of course, contain much information of interest to the topics covered here, but must be studied in its own right and on its own terms. To accommodate further interest in these materials, within the notes to each Talmudic passage I provide references to parallel materials found in the Babylonian Talmud, or Bavli.
13. Notable exceptions are Louis Ginzburg, "Introductory Essay: The Palestinian Talmud," in *A Commentary on the Palestinian Talmud: A Study of the Development of the Halakhah and Haggadah in Palestine and Babylonia*, 4 vols. (New York: Ktav, 1971; originally published 1941), vol. 1, pp. xiii–xxii; and Baruch M. Bokser, "An Annotated Bibliographical Guide to the Study of the Pal-

to do with traditional Jewish attitudes, the other with the availability of scholarly tools.

First, the Talmud of the Land of Israel has been eclipsed by its larger, but younger, sibling, the Babylonian Talmud. The "Bavli" has emerged, in the centuries since its redaction around 600 C.E. in what is today Iraq, as the paramount legal authority in Judaism. Proper legal procedure in medieval and modern Judaism reinforces this eclipse. To render legal judgment, one first consults the Bavli—or, more precisely, the medieval codes based upon it—and then turns to the Talmud of the Land of Israel only as a last resort.[14] In practice, this attitude has meant that few legal searches and references were ever made to the Talmud of the Land of Israel. Along the way, the Talmud of the Land of Israel's information on the development of Jewish thought and culture also has been ignored. That is to say, with few exceptions, rabbinic chronicles of Judaism in Israel within the first few centuries after the Mishnah's redaction have been based largely upon the Bavli's version of matters.[15] No matter that two hundred years had passed, and that the Bavli's attitudes toward history and law were formed in a different land, under a different imperial rule. The traditional Jewish preference for the Babylonian Talmud thus has contributed to ignorance of the Talmud of the Land of Israel.

Second, recent reconstructions of Jewish culture and intellectual history—which have attempted to utilize all relevant literary sources, including the Talmud of the Land of Israel—have been hampered by the lack of accessible working tools and

---

estinian Talmud," in Jacob Neusner, ed., *The Study of Ancient Judaism*, vol. 2, *The Palestinian and Babylonian Talmuds* (New York: Ktav, 1981), pp. 1–119.

14. This point has been eloquently made in fiction by Chaim Potok in *The Promise* (New York: Knopf, 1969), pp. 318–28, which displays the near apoplexy of a rabbinic authority who is confronted with a passage of the Talmud of the Land of Israel assumed by his student to be more authoritative than the parallel Bavli passage.

15. See, for example, Benjamin Menasseh Lewin, *Iggeret Rav Sherirah Gaon in der französischen und spanischen Version* (Haifa: Godah-Ittkovski, 1921). See also Gedaliah ibn Yihyah, *Shalshelet ha-Kabbalah* (Warsau: 1890).

translations of the Talmud.[16] Since historians of religion rarely have the requisite training and background in rabbinic texts, little progress has been made on using the Talmud of the Land of Israel as evidence for the attitude and mind of post-Mishnaic Judaism.[17]

Relief is in sight, however, thanks to the appearance of a new English translation of the Talmud,[18] which has opened the entire Talmud to inquiry and moved scholarship beyond mere philology to the discipline of the history of religions.[19] Throughout the following chapters, all passages of the Talmud—translated newly here from the original—may profitably be studied within the context of broader Talmudic discussion, as found in the new English edition.

Overview: The Talmud's Materials on the Ten Commandments

In the course of its essays, the Talmud of the Land of Israel devotes some fifty passages to discussion of one or another aspect of the Ten Commandments. These passages range from simple, formal use of a single verse as a prooftext, to complex historiographical observations about revelation and Israel's God. Since the relevant passages are scatterred widely through-

---

16. The first modern translation was Moise Schwab, *Le Talmud de Jérusalem*, 6 vols. (Paris: G.P. Maisonneuve, 1960).
17. But contrast Baruch Bokser, *Post Mishnaic Judaism in Transition: Samuel on Berakhot and the Beginnings of Gemara*, Brown Judaic Studies 17 (Chico, Calif.: Scholars Press, 1980). This study painstakingly reviews the textual evidence for the earliest rabbinic commentary and inquiry into the Mishnah and its legal thought.
18. Jacob Neusner et al., *The Talmud of the Land of Israel: A Preliminary Translation and Explanation*. 35 vols. (Chicago, Ill.: University of Chicago Press, 1982–   ).
19. Neusner's ambitious program is to translate or retranslate each document of the rabbinic canon, and to carry out the first layer of history of religions inquiry. For examples, see his *Judaism: The Evidence of the Mishnah; Judaism in Society; Judaism and Scripture: The Evidence of Leviticus Rabbah* (Chicago, Ill.: University of Chicago Press, 1986); and *Judaism: The Classical Statement: The Evidence of the Bavli* (Chicago, Ill.: University of Chicago Press, 1986).

out the Talmud, some overview of the Talmud's treatment of the Ten Commandments will enable better understanding of individual passages. If we know, in the main, when and why the Talmud mentions the Ten Commandments, we shall be able to make sense of a given passage more easily.

Idolatry and Transgression

As far as the individual Commandments are concerned, the Talmud's treatment is quite episodic. Not all of the Ten Commandments are invoked directly. In fact, some of the scriptural verses are never cited in the entire Talmud of the Land of Israel.[20] Such silence, especially in light of the extensive treatment of some transgressions (such as murder, mentioned above) solely in other biblical contexts, seems powerful. If rabbinic discussions proceeded apace, it was because of the secure knowledge that, for the most part, the Ten Utterances serve as reminders of laws we all should know anyway.

But when the rabbinic authors *do* mention a given Commandment, citing a verse such as "You shall not bear false witness against your neighbor," what do they wish to say? The rabbis' overwhelming tendency is to equate the transgression at hand with idolatry: "You shall have no other gods besides Me!" Bearing false witness is comparable to worshipping an idol; committing adultery is comparable to worshipping an idol. Why? The rabbis take seriously the first of God's Utterances: "I the LORD am your God who brought you out of the land of Egypt,

---

20. See Aaron Hyman, *Torah Ha-kᵊtuvah vᵊ-Ha-mᵊsurah: A Reference Book of the Scriptural Passages Quoted in Talmudic, Midrashic, and Early Rabbinic Literature*, 2d ed., rev. and enlarged by Arthur B. Hyman, 3 vols. (Tel-Aviv: Dᵊvir Publishing, 1979), which cross-references the Hebrew Bible and early rabbinic literature. For the Ten Commandments, see vol. 1, pp. 128–31, 282–83. Within the Exodus version of the Decalogue, no entries for the Talmud Yerushalmi are listed for the prohibitions against murder, adultery, or covetousness; the Deuteronomic Decalogue is cited still less widely, references lacking for the LORD as Israel's God, as well as the prohibitions against other gods, vain use of God's name, murder, adultery, and theft.

the house of bondage!" God's zealous desire to be Israel's deity, expressed positively through the special historical relationship between God and Israel, prepares the way for all that follows. Observance of God's Commandments clearly implies the Israelites' recognition of their relationship to God. But, as a corollary, ignoring any one of the Commandments would imply an idolatrous disregard: You shall have no other gods besides Me!

The Democratization of Scripture

A slightly different situation arises when we consider those Talmudic passages that take the Ten Commandments as a set or as an independent literary construction within the Hebrew Bible. I already noted Judaism's—and the Talmud's—ambivalent regard for the Ten Utterances. The twofold impulse to spend precious little time on the (absolutely central and crucial) Ten Commandments represents the rabbinic democratization of Scripture. The rabbis refuse to reduce Scripture to a single dogma, and thus are able to preserve the wholeness of Jewish law and life. As part of this whole, all verses are equally important. The rabbis, for their part, have the task of determining in a given situation how the order they find implicit in the Bible applies, and which scriptural elements predominate.[21]

This situational approach to Jewish law informs the following passage regarding the Mishnah's divorce law. Within the early rabbinic system, women who behaved outside the bounds of proper conduct could be divorced without the usual consideration, namely, payment of a settlement specified before the marriage. This passage refers to such heinous activity as "transgressing against the law of Moses or against Jewish law." Of interest here is the definition of these two categories of law not in terms of the Ten Commandments (although a few are

---

21. On the rabbinic selection of biblical materials, see Jacob Neusner, *Method and Meaning in Ancient Judaism*, 3d series (Brown Judaic Studies; Chico, Calif.: Scholars Press, 1981), pp. 15–57.

relevant), but in terms of the rabbis' own categories constructed specifically for this case.

M. Ketuvot 7:6

These [women may be] divorced without [the payment of the] marriage contract: she who transgresses against the law of Moses or against Jewish law.

What is the law of Moses? [If] she feeds [her husband food from which] tithes have not been separated, or has sexual relations with him while she is menstruating, or does not separate her dough offering, or vows and does not carry out her vow.

And what is Jewish law? If she goes out with her hair flowing loose, or she spins in the marketplace, or she talks with just anybody. Abba Saul says, "The same applies if she curses his parents in his presence." R. Ṭarfon says, "Again, the same applies if she is a loud-mouth."

The offenses for which a woman may be divorced include violation of two of the Ten Commandments: failure to fulfill a vow, presumably utilizing a divine epithet, and cursing her in-laws. These infractions, however, in no way form a category of action unto themselves, but are subsumed under two rubrics of the rabbis' innovation, "Jewish law" and "the law of Moses." The democratic principle is at work here: each of Scripture's injunctions is as important as any other, because the rabbis see them as part of an integrated whole. As a result, the rabbis can combine infractions together as they see fit.

An intricate and delicate structure links together all rules the rabbis expound. Whether clearly tied to the Hebrew Bible or merely hung from an appropriate prooftext, all of the laws—as finally laid forth by the rabbis—constitute a single whole. This excerpt shows the rabbis at their most self-conscious moment, recognizing the vast differences between various laws vis à vis Scripture, while still sensitive to the underlying coherence of the larger category of rabbinic law.

Mishnah Ḥagigah 1:8

The release of vows hovers in the air, for it has nothing [in the Torah] upon which to depend.

The laws of the Sabbath, festal offerings, and sacrilege—they are like mountains hanging by a hair, for they have little Scripture, but many laws.

Civil litigations, the sacrificial cult, things to be kept cultically clean, [sources of] cultic uncleanness, and prohibited consanguineous marriages have much on which to depend.

Yet both these and those [equally] are the essentials of the Torah.

Yerushalmi Hagigah 1:8 [Venice: 76d; Vilna:7b]

. . . R. Joshua b. Levi said, "[The precise wording with which Scripture describes Sinaitic revelation is crucial, for Deut. 9:10 states, '*Then the LORD gave me two stone tablets, written with the finger of God; and upon them was written according to all these words that the LORD spoke with you in the mountain, out of the midst of the fire on the day of assembly.*'] [Note that for] '*upon them [was written* . . .],' [Scripture reads] '*and upon them [was written* . . .]'; [for] '*all [the words* . . .],' [Scripture reads] '*according to all [the words* . . .]'; [for] '*words,*' [Scripture reads] '*these words.*' [These special formulations, including the extra particles, are meant to teach that the Torah given at Sinai included more than just the words written upon the tablets, but also] Scripture, the Mishnah, the Talmud, Law, and Lore. [All these types of law are deemed to have the authority of Sinaitic revelation.]"

[In fact, the verse implies that] even that which a learned student someday in the future will recite before his master already was transmitted to Moses on Sinai.

What reasoning [allows one to derive this point from Scripture]? "*Sometimes there is a phenomenon of which they say, 'Look, this is new!*'" (Eccles. 1:10a). His friend responds to him and says. "[There is no new teaching, for] '*It occurred long since, in ages that went before us*' (Eccles. 1:10b)."[22]

The Mishnah's image of a mountain range hung from a single hair, or even hovering totally unsupported, does capture the relationship between some major portions of rabbinic law and Scripture. Sabbath law, for example, although explicitly part of

---

22. For parallel passages, see B. Megillah 19b and B. Niddah 7b.

both the Ten Commandments and broader Pentateuchal law, was expanded so greatly by the rabbis that its biblical foundations seem only the seed from which the fruit sprung forth.

Joshua b. Levi's remarks in the Talmudic complement take this one step further: the rabbis exercised remarkable freedom in determining the active and actionable law, even according the full authority of God's revelation to mere student recitals. The authors of the Talmud of the Land of Israel sometimes downplayed given Commandments, combining them with other biblical prooftexts or rabbinic ordinances, so as to realize within their direct revealed heritage meanings that are not readily available, if available at all, to a reader uneducated in rabbinic modes of interpretation. Other times these sages expounded so many laws from a single Commandment that the simple meaning of the Sinaitic narrative is difficult to recover. Yet all rules, filtered through the rabbinic consistory, were deemed equal building blocks of "Torah," the law that defines Judaism and governs all Jews.

Authority and Miracle

Alongside this treatment of Scripture we shall find a sustained inquiry into the basis of the authoritative nature of the Ten Commandments. Once again drawing the Ten Utterances into the very center of rabbinic theology, the sages claim that God's revelation at Sinai involved miraculous speech patterns and occurrences. This notion results from seemingly insignificant differences between the two accounts of the Sinaitic revelation (Exodus versus Deuteronomy). In two cases, as we shall see in the upcoming text, a single word varies between the two scriptural passages. For the rabbis, this constitutes proof that God's voice in fact pronounced both words simultaneously and so underscores the miraculous—and authoritative—status of the Ten Commandments.

Yerushalmi Nedarim 3:2 [Venice: 36d; Vilna: 9a–b]

"[*You shall not swear] falsely* (la-shav) *by the name of the* LORD *your God*" (Deut. 5:11). "*You shall not take in vain* (la-sheqer) *the name of the* LORD *your God"* (Exod. 20:7)—both of them were stated in a single act of speech, which it is not possible for a mortal mouth to speak or a mortal ear to hear.

"Remember (zakhor) *[the sabbath day and keep it holy]"* (Exod. 20:8). *"Observe* (shamor) *[the sabbath day and keep it holy]"* (Deut. 5:12)—both of them were stated in a single act of speech, which it is not possible for a mortal mouth to speak or a mortal ear to hear.

. . . And so too Scripture says:*"One thing God has spoken; two things I have heard; [that might belongs to God]"* (Ps. 62:12).

And it is written: *"Behold My word is like fire—declares the LORD—and like a hammer that shatters rock!"* (Jer. 23:29).

The crucial interpretive step for the rabbis is reading the two versions of the Decalogue with Psalm 62:12 clearly in mind: "One thing God has spoken; two things I have heard; that might belongs to God." This marks the Ten Utterances as truly divine and as wielding divine authority.

Rabbinic attention to, and discussion of, the Ten Commandments is sporadic, evidence that the centerpiece of the Sinai narratives simply did not matter that much to these authorities. This decentralizing force finds ready expression in the rabbis' creative categorization of law, subsuming some of the Ten Utterances, leaving out others.

Just as characteristic, however, is the rabbis' assertion that God's exclusive linguistic abilities stand behind the Ten Commandments, accentuating the whole as one of the categories (if not the crucial category) of true revelation. And the point of that revelation, as clearly stated in the opening passages of the Utterances, is to promote Israel's relationship to the one God and to prohibit idolatry.

3. In Search of the Rabbinic Agenda within Scripture

Judaism often is referred to as a religion of the book, namely, the Hebrew Bible. Basic Jewish teachings and folktales are contained in the Bible, alongside the foundations of the Jewish ethical system. But what reality did Scripture hold for the rabbis who wrote the Talmud of the Land of Israel? Were they biblical fundamentalists or innovative lawyers? Or did their understanding of Scripture develop an approach unique unto itself, which such modern categories of interpretation do not adequately express?

In characterizing the Judaic approach to Scripture, the Ten Commandments prove an interesting test case. As mentioned above, not all of the verses of the Ten Commandments are invoked in Talmudic literature, and the Decalogue itself is not subjected to prolonged, systematic analysis. In this respect, questions regarding the usage of these biblical verses parallel precisely other topical investigations brought to Talmudic literature. For example, the rabbis of the Talmud likewise composed no single comprehensive essay on categories such as Torah or Creation. Drawing on scattered usages, then, we embark on a theological enterprise, noting how the rabbis create statements of faith and belief through oblique references. By looking at the various relationships the rabbis strike up with the biblical Ten Commandments, we shall see illustrated the broader relationship of nascent rabbinism to its biblical antecedents. That relationship is rich indeed.

The Bible's Relevance (and Irrelevance)

If the Hebrew Bible does not alone characterize Judaism, that is little wonder. An intricate web is spun within the halakhic process, sometimes emphasizing biblical foundations, at other times creating legal precedent. In their literature, the rabbis demonstrate that the Bible's materials fall across a wide range, from fully relevant to rather inconsequential.

On the side of relevance, typical rabbinic methodology *does* begin with an assessment of scriptural precedent. Hence, when taking up complex issues of law or values, the rabbis move chronologically, from most authoritative, Sinaitic materials (attributed to direct revelation from God), on through to laws with lesser status, including most of the rabbinic teachings. The Talmud distinguishes laws that are scriptural (*mi-dᵊ-oraita*) from those that are rabbinic enactments (*mi-dᵊ-rabbanan*), and usually assigns precedence to the former.

The Talmud itself holds some laws to be based directly on the written Torah given to Moses on Sinai; other regulations have the authority of the rabbinic consistory that decided upon them and promulgated them. One theory of the law's development was that each generation had progressively less of an authoritative voice, since it stood a bit farther removed from the experience of Sinaitic revelation. Knowledge decreased with passing time; impulses toward sinful transgression increased. Within such an entropic view, little room was left for the freedom of the human intellect. Limits imposed by divine decree were the only bulwarks against forgetful transgression.

Yet in speaking of the sources of its authority, the Talmud has always engaged its students in the process of applying one set of principles—those specified in the Bible—to new and unpredicted circumstances. So it is that as the halakhic tradition matured, some balance was struck between the revealed, divine decree and the need for rational application. At times human reason took on a role equal to, or even greater then, that accorded to Sinaitic revelation, thus rendering the biblical legacy, in one sense, at least partially irrelevant.

Intensive study and analysis of the Torah over long periods of time encourage a sense of intellectual autonomy. Accomplished students of the Torah feel confident that their creative interpretation of the law is an integral part of God's original creation. . . . Torah sages are very careful readers. Their unqualified respect and love for the literal meaning of each word of the Torah is, paradoxically, what accounts for their enormous confidence in delving below the surface and addressing themselves to the undisclosed spirit and intention of the Word.[1]

Within Judaism, the most noble and best of all activities is to engage in studying the law. People have a clear duty to complement the written and oral law—the Hebrew Bible, Mishnah, and Talmuds—with their own interpretation and explanation. That use of the intellect prevents entropy from destroying the legal system. By infusing the legal process with a few necessary, final ingredients, students of rabbinism transform degeneration to development, and thereby create a progressive law.

In order to clarify the halakhic approach to a given question, we must keep in mind this balance between legal degeneration and human progress. What are the scriptural foundations of the law? What are rabbinic additions or deletions? When and why do the legal sages allow and foster change? What priorities are assigned to specific biblical and rabbinic regulations? Each of these questions reflects on the theory of authority that underlies the halakhic system. Understanding these varied sources of law in turn allows apprehension of, and participation in, the processes of Jewish law.

Rabbinic Reasoning and Scriptural Warrant: Prooftexting

Most characteristic of the relationship between these two poles—revelation at Sinai as against human reason acting independently—stands the rabbis' careful attempts to show the two in perfect coordination.

Linkage between the Written Torah and the rabbis' rulings is most often accomplished through the use of prooftexts. A passage will state the law as the rabbis establish it, then show carefully what verses of Scripture might serve as a foundation for the law. Similarly, a Talmudic unit might systematically

---

1. David Hartmann, *A Living Covenant*, p. 41.

work through a biblical citation, explaining phrase by phrase the unstated details and assumptions of the law. Not all prooftexts are alike, however, as far as their relevance to the topic under discussion by the rabbis. The Talmudic materials that now follow draw prooftexts from the Decalogue. But in the rabbis' attempt to coordinate their own statements regarding the Ten Utterances with the Decalogue of the Written Torah, they show us a range of uses for biblical texts: a given verse might be cited as an antecedent law, as the basis for a legal investigation of analogy, or finally omitted altogether as insignificant.

Prooftexts I: Sources and Antecedents.

The first type of prooftext-unit, illustrated here three times, treats a verse from the Decalogue as directly relevant. These units typically address a matter of rabbinic interest, such as delineation of the punishment incurred for violating the law. Such inquiries are then answered through simple references to verses of Scripture, claimed to be the origin of (or at least an implicit nod toward) the law under study.

The opening passage takes up two of the Ten Utterances, namely, Sabbath observance and parental honor, and addresses to each a single line of questioning.

Mishnah Sanhedrin 7:8

I. *One who profanes the Sabbath [is to be executed by stoning* (cf. M. San. 7:4)]—this refers to an act for which one incurs extirpation if [the transgression] is deliberate, but merely a sin offering if inadvertent.

II. *One who curses his father and his mother [is to be executed by stoning* (cf. M. San 7:4)]—[this refers to a case] in which one cursed them using the divine Name. [If] one cursed them with a euphemism, R. Meir declares one liable. But sages declare [the same person] exempt. . . .

Yerushalmi Sanhedrin 7:11 [Venice: 25c; Vilna: 39b-40a]

Whence do we derive a warning against profaning [the Sabbath]? *"[The seventh day is a sabbath of the* LORD *your God:] you shall not do any work"* (Exod. 20:10).

Whence do we derive [the penalty of] extirpation? *"Whoever does work on it, that person shall be cut off from among his kin"* (Exod. 31: 14b). Whence do we derive a [court-administered] punishment? *"He who profanes it shall be put to death"* (Exod. 31:14a). . . .

Whence do we find a warning against cursing one's father and mother? *"Every person shall revere his mother and his father"* (Lev. 19:3). Whence do we derive both the [court-administered] penalty and extirpation? *"He who insults his father or his mother shall be put to death"* (Exod. 21:17), [implies the death penalty]. And [when Scripture] says, *"All who do any of these abhorrent things—such people shall be cut off from their people"* (Lev. 18:29), [it implies divine extirpation].[2]

Here the coordination of rabbinic interest and Scripture's words is explicit. The Talmud's authors have in mind two principles, namely, that God has warned the Israelite community about the laws at hand, and that transgression ought to imply twofold punishment, at the hands of a rabbinic court and through divine destruction. These two assertions are logically primary to this prooftexting exercise, a fact made clear by the repeating redactional structure within the passage.

In order to ground these assertions in the Written Torah and to lend them authority, the rabbis refer to the Ten Commandments and other relevant biblical verses. In the case of Sabbath law, God's direct command in the Decalogue is central, supplemented by a later biblical specification of punishment. The prohibition against cursing one's parents is a slightly different matter, if only because it refers in fact to the inverse of the Fifth Commandment (a prohibition against *cursing,* rather than an obligation to *honor,* one's parents). Accordingly, the rabbis cite not the Decalogue itself, but more immediately relevant verses.

The next prooftext passage presents a similar exercise in searching for biblical foundations. The Talmud's attention here is drawn to the Eighth Commandment, the prohibition against

---

2. For parallel passages, see B. Sanhedrin 53a, B. Shabbat 153b–154a, B. Shevuot 35a, and B. Ketuvot 49a.

theft, by a Mishnaic unit dealing with a rebellious and incorrigible child who steals from his own parents. The mere mention of stealing gives the Talmud's authors an opportunity to discuss theft in general; here they distinguish theft of objects (mere robbery) from theft of human beings (kidnapping). As before, this distinction gives rise to a short foray into biblical antecedents, alleging that the Written Torah itself refers separately to kidnapping and robbery.

Yerushalmi Sanhedrin 8:3 [Venice: 26b; Vilna: 42a]

Whence do we derive a warning against the first [type of] stealing [namely, kidnapping]? "You shall not steal" (Exod. 20:13).

Whence do we derive a warning against the second [type of] stealing [namely, theft of property]? "You [pl.] shall not steal" (Lev. 19:11).

[The use of a plural verb at Lev. 19:11 indicates two separate aspects of this command:] [The first] "You shall not steal" [prohibits taking an item temporarily] for spite, [even if one has the intention to return the item later]. [The second] "You shall not steal" [prohibits converting someone else's property to one's own use, even if one has the intention] to pay double compensation or fourfold or fivefold damages.

Ben Bag-Bag says, "[The verse's plural means that people must avoid duplicating theft.] [That is,] you shall not "re-steal" your own property from a thief, lest you appear to be a thief."[3]

Here the Bible's duplication of a simple command—"You shall not steal"—generates the rabbinic distinction: since no word of Torah should be considered repetitious, these two verses must refer to different types of theft. Likewise, the plural imperative at Leviticus 9:11 implies a double message, as explained by Ben Bag-Bag and anonymously. The rabbis' desire to coordinate their rules with Scripture therefore extends even to careful note of linguistic usage.

The third and final example of a prooftext directly related to one of the Ten Commandments again regards Sabbath law, al-

---

3. For parallel passages, see B. Sanhedrin 86a–b, B. Bava Qamma 27b, and B. Bava Meṣia 61b.

though the prooftext itself is largely trivial. The Mishnah provides a list of rules to be applied equally to all animals, and the Talmud simply gives the scriptural verses relevant to each law.

Mishnah Bava Qamma 5:7

All the same are an ox and all other beasts so far as (1) falling into a pit, (2) keeping apart from Mount Sinai, (3) a double indemnity, (4) the returning of that which is lost, (5) unloading, (6) muzzling, (7) hybridization, and (8) the Sabbath.

And so too, wild beasts and fowl are subject to the same laws.

If so, why does [Scripture] specify [only] "an ox or an ass"? Because Scripture spoke in terms of prevailing conditions.

Yerushalmi Bava Qamma 5:8 [Venice: 5a; Vilna: 26a]

. . . As to the Sabbath, [what prooftext speaks only of "an ox or an ass"]? *"[You shall not do any work]—* . . . *that your ox or your ass . . . may rest [as you do]"* (Deut. 5:14).

In the three instances just examined, the Talmud cited a verse from the Ten Commandments in response to its primary question: what is the source or legal antecedent for a rabbinic concept? As I indicated, merely asking this question illustrates the Talmudic authors' desire to show their conceptions to be in line with God's Sinaitic revelation. Scripture thus serves as a tool of rabbinic theology, showing the integrity of the entire legal system, both Written Torah and Oral Law.

Prooftext II: Tangential Comparison and Contrast

A second type of prooftext unit now requires some illustration. Here a verse of the Ten Utterances is used rhetorically, merely to establish or conclude a comparison and contrast between two barely relevant laws. Such a use of Scripture cedes little to biblical authority. Rather, in this instance, rabbinic logical association issues in a transitory reference to a biblical verse.

The Talmud's materials on the Ten Utterances contain one straightforward example of this type of prooftext, which contrasts two quite diverse laws, those governing writs of divorce and the Sabbath. At issue throughout this passage is a question of personal domain. Does the airspace surrounding a person or object constitute part of the person's or object's own private space, or is it part of the public domain? Jacob Neusner comments: "Once the basic point is made about [the delivery of a divorce writ into] the contained airspace of the roof, the secondary expansion moves on to compare the law of the Sabbath with the present one, so far as the principles of contained airspace are concerned."[4] While the topic is a bit arcane, we shall see a verse regarding the Sabbath invoked at the end entirely tangentially vis à vis public and private domains.

Mishnah Giṭṭin 8:3

[If the wife about to be divorced] was standing on the rooftop and he threw [the divorce writ] to her, then from the moment it entered the airspace of the roof, the woman is divorced.

[If] he is up above [on the roof] and she is below [on the ground] and he threw [the divorce decree] to her, then from the moment it has left the domain of the roof the woman is divorced, [even if the decree] should be blotted out or burned up [before she receives it].

Yerushalmi Giṭṭin 8:3 [Venice: 49c; Vilna: 46a–b]

Said R. Eleazar, "[With reference to a case in which the wife is standing on the rooftop,] the Mishnah deals with a rooftop surrounded by a parapet." [The divorce is enacted, therefore,] when [the writ] has fallen into the contained airspace of the parapet.

In the case of a rooftop lacking a parapet, [the divorce is enacted] when [the writ] has fallen into the airspace within three cubits of the roof. For three cubits of airspace nearest to the roof are deemed tantamount to the roof itself.

R. Jacob bar Aḥa, R. Ba bar Hamnuna in the name of R. Ada bar Ahva, "Along these same lines [is the law prohibiting one to carry an item from one domain into another] on the Sabbath. For the three

---

4. Neusner, *Talmud of the Land of Israel*, vol. 25, *Gittin*, p. 212.

cubits nearest a suspended partition are deemed tantamount to the partition. [That is to say, if a partition reaches to within three cubits of the ground, it fully delineates a separate domain vis-à-vis Sabbath carrying.]"

[Arguing against any comparison between the two laws,] said R. Yosa, "But the matter of [throwing] a writ of divorce upwards is not parallel to the matter of [extending a partition] downwards [as to the law regarding carrying on] the Sabbath. With regard to a divorce decree: even if it did not come to rest [but merely entered the roof's airspace], the divorce is granted. [But] with regard to [violating the prohibition against carrying from one domain to another on] the Sabbath, [an item] must [actually] come to rest [within a domain marked off by a suspended partition]. . . . "

. . . What [scriptural prootexts indicate] the difference between [the law governing] writs of divorce and [the law governing] the Sabbath?

Said R. Abba, "In regard to the Sabbath, it is written, 'You shall not do any work' (Exod. 20:10), could this be accomplished merely up [above the ground]? But with regard to the present matter, [Scripture states], '[He writes her a bill of divorcement,] hands it to her . . . ' (Deut. 24:1)—that is, [he places it] anywhere in her domain."[5]

In this type of unit, Scripture is invoked merely to substantiate a well-established rabbinic ruling, here spelling out the differences between rules of domain applicable to receipt of items as against carrying on the Sabbath. This unit validates the divergent rabbinic rulings by allusion to incongruous formulations in Scripture itself. Yet the citation of the Fourth Commandment here is not in and of itself the genesis of the rabbinic distinction, but figures in the discussion only because the issue at hand (personal domain) may be explained additionally with respect to Sabbath law. This is in rather sharp contrast to the earlier cases, in which the prooftext played a central role in the Talmud's argument, constituting the bulk of the passages at hand.

Prooftexts III: Omissions

An approach that accords a less central role to the Ten Utterances and relies instead on a different scriptural passage is the

---

5. For a parallel passage, see B. Giṭṭin 49a–b.

final type of prooftext unit. Here the rabbis address a topic related to the Ten Utterances, namely, murder. The subject arises in the Talmudic treatment of an ox that causes a person's death by knocking down a wall. But as we shall see, this discussion of murder has no place whatsoever for the Sixth Commandment, "You shall not murder." Instead, the rabbis cite a different verse, from Leviticus, to begin their discussion of the topic.

Mishnah Bava Qamma 4:6

[As regards] an ox that was rubbing up against a wall, so that [the wall] fell [and killed] a person: [if the ox] had intended to kill another beast, but killed a person; an idol-worshipper, but killed an Israelite; an untimely birth, but killed a viable infant—[the ox] is exempt.

Yerushalmi Bava Qamma 4:6 [Venice: 4c; Vilna: 22a]

"If anyone kills any human being, [he shall be put to death]" (Lev. 24:17). This encompasses any case in which one strikes another with sufficient force to cause death, [even if the deathblow is a mere tap].

There are Tannaitic authorities who teach [that the verse encompasses one who strikes another] without sufficient force to cause death, [if the blow was delivered to an already dying person]. Said R. La, "[That is to say: if one strikes another] with sufficient force to cause death, but then another person delivers the *coup de grace* [which alone would not have caused death], the one who actually killed the person [that is, the latter] is liable."[6]

The three ways in which the rabbis utilize prooftexts when discoursing on the Ten Utterances demonstrate the remarkable range of the Bible's potential use. At times an entire passage is constructed in the Talmud merely to showcase a verse from the Decalogue in contrast to some other biblical reference to the same law. At the other extreme, just exemplified, the relevant verse from the Ten Utterances was not cited at all. Midway between this typology are those prooftexts that establish a bridge from one topic to another, tangentially related, issue.

---

6. For a parallel passage, see B. Sanhedrin 78a.

In any case, these examples of prooftexts drawn from the Ten Commandments serve well to illustrate a broad rabbinic approach to biblical theology. One paramount Talmudic interest—exemplified here for the case of the Decalogue, but true in general as well—is to coordinate the two Torahs. The Oral Law (that is, the Mishnah and Talmud) is carefully brought into focus through the lens of the Written Torah.[7] When a biblical topic arises, be it Sabbath law or prohibitions against theft or murder, the rabbis quickly point out the scriptural antecedents for their rulings, simply applied to updated circumstances.

A Systematic Treatment of the Ten Utterances: *Mekhilta de-Rabbi Ishmael*

The Talmud's treatment of biblical materials through prooftexts is far from systematic, at least as far as the Decalogue is concerned. In fact, the Talmud has no extended essay on the Ten Utterances, whether proceeding verse by verse or one topic at a time. Of course, this lack of a systematic treatment within the Talmud need not mean that rabbinic thinkers failed to grasp the whole of which each Commandment was a part.

In order to appreciate the spirit behind the rabbinic approach to Scripture, we need to see what a systematic treatment would look like. Just such a theological essay can be found in *Mekhilta de-Rabbi Ishmael*, a midrashic (exegetical) text composed in Israel roughly contemporaneously to the Talmud.[8] *Mekhilta's* materials

---

7. This coordination is especially true of the Talmud of the Land of Israel. See Neusner, *Judaism in Society*, pp. 78–89.
8. Two English translations of *Mekhilta de-Rabbi Ishmael* are available. The first is a rather poetic work: Jacob Z. Lauterbach, *Mekilta de-Rabbi Ishmael: A Critical Edition on the Basis of the Manuscripts and Early Editions with an English Translation, Introduction, and Notes*, 3 vols. (Philadelphia, Pa.: Jewish Publication Society, 1933–1935). The second is a syntactically analytic version: Jacob Neusner, *Mekhilta according to Rabbi Ishmael: An Analytic Translation*, 2 vols. (Atlanta, Ga.: Scholars Press, 1988). Parallels to this essay are found episodically in *Pesikhta de-Rav Kahana*, especially chapter 21.

on the Ten Commandments are systematic in two separate ways: first, this passage of Midrash takes each verse of the Decalogue in Exodus one by one, presenting ample expansion of the Bible's language and ideas. Second, the essay as a whole utilizes formal, redactional, and substantive clues to make a larger claim: while interpersonal duties pale in comparison to those that obligate people before God, both are equally part of the great Sinaitic legacy. Both formally and substantively, then, the midrashic discourse expresses the spirit of the theological principle that the rabbinic interpreters assumed.

Mekhilta's essay on the Decalogue is extensive, occupying four full chapters (Baḥodesh 5–9). In order to illustrate its programmatic treatment of the Decalogue, I shall present excerpts that highlight the larger redactional message. For example, *Mekhilta*'s treatment of the Ten Utterances opens with wide ranging attention to the first five Commandments, which specify duties before the Omnipresent. The midrashic materials here cover a vast range of inquiries, averaging between ten and twelve separate units of discourse for each Commandment. Consider as representative the following expansion of the First Commandment:

First Commandment: I the LORD am your God (Mekhilta Baḥodesh 5)

I. "*I the LORD am your God [who brought you out of the land of Egypt, the house of bondage]*" (Exod. 20:2).

Why weren't the Ten Utterances stated at the very beginning of the Torah? The matter may be compared to the case of a person who entered a city, and said, "I shall rule over you!" The [inhabitants of the city] said to him, "You haven't done anything to [earn the right] to rule us." What did he then do? He built a city wall, [aqueducts to] bring water, and led them in battles. [Again] he declared "I shall rule over you!" and they responded, "Yes, indeed."

Similarly, the Omnipresent brought the Israelites out of Egypt, divided the Red Sea, provided *manna* [for food], maintained wellsprings, gave them quail, and made war against Amaleq. Then [God] said to them, "I shall rule over you!" and they responded, "Yes, indeed."

II. Rabbi says, "[This verse] expresses the praise owing to the Israelites. For when they all stood before Mount Sinai to receive the Torah, they joyfully and unanimously subjugated themselves to Heavenly dominion. Furthermore, they exacted pledges from one another."

III. When the Holy, Blessed One made a covenant with them, [the Holy One] revealed [rules for communal responsibility for] not only overt, but also private acts. They said to him, "We agree to a covenant with you concerning [communal responsibility for] public acts, but not that which is done in secret, lest an individual commit a sin in private and the entire community bear responsibility."

[Thus Scripture states], *"Concealed acts concern the LORD our God; but with overt acts, it is for us and our children [ever to apply all the provisions of this Teaching]"* (Deut. 29:28).

IV. *"I the LORD am your God:"*

Why is this stated? Because [God] appeared at the sea as a mighty soldier—as [Scripture] says, *"The LORD, the Warrior"* (Exod. 15:3). But [God] appeared at Mount Sinai as a merciful elder—as [Scripture] says, *"And they saw the God of Israel: [under (God's) feet there was the likeness of a pavement of sapphire,] like the very sky for purity"* (Exod. 24:10). And [Scripture further] describes [God], *"As I looked on, thrones were set in place [and the Ancient of Days took the seat] . . . "* (Dan. 7:9). And it says, *"A river of fire streamed forth before [God] . . . "* (Dan. 7:10).

Therefore, so as not to give the nations of the world a chance to say that there were two Dominions, [Scripture says], *"I the LORD am your God"*—"I was in Egypt; I was at the sea; I was at Sinai; I was in the past; I will be in the future; I am in this world and I will be in the world-to-come!" As it is written [in Scripture], *"See, then, that I, I am [LORD]; [There is no god beside Me]"* (Deut. 32:39); *"Till you grow old, I will still be the same"* (Isa. 46:4); *"Thus says the LORD, the King of Israel, their Redeemer, the LORD of Hosts: I am the first and I am the last"* (Isa. 44:6); *"Who has wrought and achieved this? The One who announced the generations from the start—I, the LORD, who was first and will be with the last as well"* (Isa. 41:4).

R. Nathan says, "Thus do we refute the *minim,* who maintain that there are two Dominions. When the Holy, Blessed One said, '*I the LORD am your God [who brought you out of the land of Egypt, the house of bondage],*' [was there any other power] to oppose [God]? And if you maintain that this Utterance was made in secret, is it not stated, '*I did not speak in secret, [at a site in a land of darkness]; I did not say to the children of Jacob, "Seek Me out in a wasteland"'* (Isa. 45:19): 'Did I not give it in public?' And so [Scripture states], 'I *the* LORD, *who foretells reliably, who announces what is true'* (Isa. 45:19)."

The treatment of the First Commandment alone continues in *Mekhilta* for another twenty-three units, the whole occupying 158 lines in the Horowitz-Rabin critical edition.[9] This abundant commentary and the rabbis' painstaking detail in word-by-word expansion underscore the importance attached to the First Commandment, establishing the exclusive relation between God and Israel. The other theological Commandments—the prohibitions against graven images of God or using God's name in vain, and the obligations to observe God's Sabbath and to honor God's surrogates, one's parents—are just as extensive. The message of *Mekhilta's* editors thus far is clear: the theological duties loom large, raising important questions and issues, each requiring careful interpretation and explanation.

If we next turn to *Mekhilta's* passages on the interpersonal norms, matters will be seen entirely differently. The scriptural prohibitions against murder, adultery, theft, perjury, and covetousness are treated almost trivially. In the following units— presented in full for contrast to the preceding—note how the brief treatment reveals that *Mekhilta's* editors had few questions, little interest. The only query asked with any precision is how to derive from Scripture both a warning against transgression and the penalty for failure to heed that warning.

Sixth Commandment: You shall not murder (Mekhilta Baḥodesh 8)

I. *"You shall not murder"* (Exod. 20:13)—

Why is this stated? Since it is said, *"Whoever sheds the blood of a human by humanity shall his blood be shed"* (Gen. 9:6), we may derive the pen-

---

9. H. S. Horowitz and Y. A. Rabin, *Mekhilta de-Rabbi Yishmael: With Variant Readings and Notes*, 2d ed. (Jerusalem: Wahrmann, 1960), pp. 219–27.

alty. How shall we derive Scripture's warning? The verse teaches: *"You shall not murder."*

Seventh Commandment: You shall not commit adultery (Mekhilta Baḥodesh 8, continued)

I. *"You shall not commit adultery"* (Exod. 20:13)—

Why is this stated? Since it is said, *"The adulterer and the adulteress shall be put to death"* (Lev. 20:10), we may derive the penalty. How shall we derive Scripture's warning? The verse teaches: *"You shall not commit adultery."*

Eighth Commandment: You shall not steal (Mekhilta Baḥodesh 8, continued)

I. *"You shall not steal"* (Exod. 20:13)—

Why is this stated? Since it is said, *"He who kidnaps a man—whether he has sold him [or is still holding him—shall be put to death]"* (Lev. 20:10), we may derive the penalty. How shall we derive Scripture's warning? The verse teaches: *"You shall not steal."*

II. Of course, this is Scripture's warning against stealing a person.

Might one say [that the Eighth Commandment] refers not to stealing a person but to stealing property? When Scripture says, *"You shall not steal"* (Lev. 19:11), that constitutes Scripture's warning against stealing property. So how then to interpret [the Eighth Commandment], *"You shall not steal"*? This is Scripture's warning against stealing a person.

Might [matters be reversed, so that] this is Scripture's warning against stealing property, while the other passage warns against stealing a person? In answer you could say: Go and derive [which verse is which] from the thirteen principles by which the Torah is interpreted,[10] [one of which states that Scripture must be interpreted in context]. In the [one verse of the Decalogue], there are three religious duties, two of them explicit, one of them implicit; we must interpret the implicit from the explicit.

---

10. On the thirteen principles of rabbinic interpretation, see chapter 4 of this volume.

Just as the two that are explicit [i.e., murder and adultery] are religious duties whose violators incur the death penalty at the hand of an earthly court, so too the one that is implicit must be a religious duty whose violators incur the death penalty at the hand of an earthly court. Accordingly, you cannot propose the second possibility, [that the Decalogue refers to theft of property, for that is not a capital crime]; but the first possibility is correct: the [Decalogue's] rule prohibits stealing a person, while the other prohibits stealing property.

Ninth Commandment: You shall not bear false witness (Mekhilta Baḥodesh 8, continued)

I. *"You shall not bear false witness against your neighbor"* (Exod. 20:13)—

Why is this stated? Since it is said, *"[If the man who testified is a false witness . . .] you shall do to him as he schemed to do to his fellow"* (Deut. 19:18–19), we may derive the penalty. How shall we derive Scripture's warning? The verse teaches: *"You shall not bear false witness against your neighbor."*

Tenth Commandment: You shall not covet (Mekhilta Baḥodesh 8, continued)

I. *"You shall not covet [your neighbor's house: you shall not covet your neighbor's wife, or his male or female slave, or his ox or his ass, or anything that is your neighbor's]"* (Exod. 20:14)—

Rabbi says, "One verse of Scripture [in Exodus' Decalogue] says, 'You shall not covet [your neighbor's wife],' while the other verse [in Deuteronomy's Decalogue] says, 'You shall not desire [your neighbor's wife]' (Deut. 5:18). How might we harmonize these two verses? [Deuteronomy's Decalogue uses the variations in language] to warn a person against desiring to profit through another's covetousness.

II. *"You shall not covet your neighbor's house . . . "*—this is a generalization; " . . . [you shall not covet your neighbor's wife], or his male or female slave, or his ox or his ass . . . "—these are particularizations. In any case of a general rule followed by specific details, the general rule may be applied only to these details. But Scripture then goes on to say, " . . . *or anything that is your neighbor's,*" which once again presents a generalization. [The question is how broadly the original statement—you shall not covet your neighbor's house—is to be taken.]

Perhaps the latter generalization has the same force as the former generalization, [in fact negating the specific details, so that any type of covetousness is prohibited]? You must answer "no." Rather, the return to a generalization gives us a general rule, followed by specific details, followed by a general rule, in which case one must adjudicate in line with the broader importance of the details provided. So, just as the details specified relate to things that may be bought and sold, so the general rule relates only to things that may be bought and sold.

Might one propose that the broader importance of the specific details is that they relate to chattels, which cannot serve as a pledge [for any debt], so that the general rule [against coveting] applies only to chattels? [No!] Since Deuteronomy in its details specifies *"his field,"* [which is real property, not chattels,] by force of reason you must agree that, just as the details specified relate to things that may be bought and sold, so the general rule relates only to things that may be bought and sold.

Might one propose that the broader importance of the specific details is that they relate to items that come into one's domain only with the owner's consent, so that the general rule [against coveting] applies only to items that come into one's domain only with the owner's consent? [No!] For that understanding would exclude your coveting his daughter for your son or his son for your daughter.

Might one propose that the commandment includes expressing covetousness through mere words? [No!] For Scripture states, *"You shall not covet the silver and gold on them and keep it for yourselves"* (Deut. 7:25). Just as in that passage one incurs liability only when one actually commits an act, so here too one is liable only if one actually commits an act.[11]

---

11. Manuscripts erroneously place this discussion of the Tenth Commandment after the essay on coordinating the Ten Utterances; see Horowitz and Rabin, *Mekhilta de-Rabbi Yishmael,* p. 233, note to line 9. See also Neusner, *Mekhilta,* p. 87, who comments: "This elegant construction is parachuted down, with no bearing on the exposition of a particular verse or phrase. We now revert to the more familiar mode of discourse: phrase-by-phrase amplification or paraphrase."

These units, on the interpersonal Commandments, prove a stunning contrast to the excerpts from the First Commandment, presented above. The clear conclusion is that ethical obligations, adjuring proper action toward others, simply do not have the status of God-centered duties. For the most part, ethical actions are perfectly clear, and thus require no theological exposition. So *Mekhilta's* editors spell out what each prohibition is and what penalties might be incurred, but little else. The theological commandments, by contrast, are all-important to *Mekhilta's* editors, and issue forth in a myriad of interesting conceptions.

But it is *Mekhilta's* final unit that draws together all of the foregoing and expresses the theological bottom line. By discussing the precise layout of the Ten Utterances on the parallel tablets, and by conceptually connecting each theological Commandment with the coordinate ethical duty, the rabbis state their commitment to *all* of the laws, given as a whole.

Mekhilta Baḥodesh 8, continued

In what arrangement were the Ten Commandments given?[12] There were five on one tablet, and five on the other.

I. On the one was written, *"I the LORD am your God,"* and opposite it, *"You shall not murder"*—Scripture thus teaches that whoever sheds blood is regarded by Torah as if he had diminished the image of the divine King.

The matter may be compared to a human king who entered a city, where the people set up icons, made statues, and minted coins in his honor. Some time later, they overturned his icons, broke his statues, and mutilated his coins, thereby diminishing the image of the king. So, whoever sheds blood is regarded by Torah as if he had diminished the image of the divine King, for it is said, *"Whoever sheds the blood of a human, [by humanity shall his blood be shed;] for in [God's] image did God make man"* (Gen. 9:6).

---

12. A laconic parallel to this unit is found at Y. Soṭah 8:3.

II. On the one was written, "*You shall have no other gods,*" and opposite it, "*You shall not commit adultery*"—Scripture thus teaches that whoever worships an object of foreign worship is regarded by Torah as if he had committed adultery against the Omnipresent, for it is said, "*You were like the adulterous wife who welcomes strangers instead of her husband*" (Ezek. 16:32); "*The LORD said to me further, 'Go, befriend a woman who, while befriended by a companion, consorts with others, [just as the LORD befriends the Israelites, but they turn to other gods and love the cups of the grape'*" (Hos. 3:1).

III. On the one was written, "*You shall not swear falsely by the name of the LORD your God,*" and opposite it, "*You shall not steal*"—Scripture thus teaches that whoever steals will eventually be led to take a false oath. For Scripture states, "*Will you steal and murder and commit adultery and swear falsely?*" (Jer. 7:9); "*False swearing, dishonesty, and murder, and theft and adultery are rife*" (Hos. 4:2).

IV. On the one was written, "*Remember the Sabbath day and keep it holy,*" and opposite it, "*You shall not bear false witness*"—Scripture thus teaches that whoever violates the Sabbath is as though he had testified that the One-Who-Spoke-and-Brought-the-World-into-Being did not create this world in six days and rest on the seventh. But whoever keeps the Sabbath is as though he testified that the One-Who-Spoke-and-Brought-the-World-into-Being did create this world in six days and rest on the seventh. As Scripture says, "*My witnesses are you—declares the LORD— . . . before Me no god was formed, and after Me none shall exist*" (Isa. 43:10).

V. On the one was written, "*Honor your father and your mother,*" and opposite it, "*You shall not covet*"—Scripture thus teaches that whoever covets eventually will raise a son who curses his father and mother, but honors one who is not his father.

VI. "Thus the Ten Commandments were given, five on this tablet, and five on that," the words of R. Ḥaninah b. Gamaliel. But sages say, "The ten [commandments from Exodus] were written on this tablet, and the ten [from Deuteronomy] on the other. For it says, '*The LORD spoke these words. . . . [The LORD] inscribed them upon two tablets of stone*' (Deut. 5:19); '*Your breasts are like two fawns, twins of a gazelle, [browsing among the lilies]*' (Song of Sol. 4:5); '*His hands are rods of gold, [double]-studded with beryl*' (Song of Sol. 5:15)."

Looking back at the whole of *Mekhilta*'s material, the systematic point is easy to discern: our duties before God are the source of our humane duties. The two sets of obligations are entirely coordinated. Humanity requires both types of law in order to balance one sphere of life with the other. The Torah comprises ethical and theological duties in equal measure. There is little need to argue how different such a programmatic essay is from that which we find in the Talmud. The Talmudic authors' silence in this regard poses a sharp contrast to the speech of Mekhilta's editors. But this only confirms that beyond the text of the Talmud was a spirit that directed rabbinic inquiry.

Like the Talmud's prooftexting materials, *Mekhilta*'s message in this essay exemplifies a more general rabbinic belief: just as one must coordinate the Written Torah, directly given by God, to the Oral Law, carried and preserved by humanity, so, too, one must balance all divine and humane duties. Hints toward this balance are found throughout rabbinic literature, including the Talmud itself.

Some laws—those in the ethical realm—are understood to govern interpersonal relationships (*miṣvot beyn adam lᵊ-ḥavero*). These include civil and social laws, prohibitions against theft, murder, fraud, and the like. Other regulations—more properly theological—aim at establishing a proper relationship between humanity and God (*miṣvot beyn adam lᵊ-maqom*), including ritual and cultic laws, but also rules for proper modes and attitudes for worship and enjoyment of divine gifts, and prohibitions against idolotry.

Of course, as Jewish jurists weigh the extent of an individual's responsibility to others, particularly in light of the relationship Jews have established with God, they reveal the underlying cultural and political assumptions of the halakhic system.

The Web of Law: In Praise of Casuistry

The rabbinic use of Scripture thus involves consideration of various structural issues from a variety of perspectives. As I spelled out above, these include consideration of the source of one's obligations, whether scriptural or rabbinic, as well as a unified approach to ethical and theological reflection. The halakhic process as a whole then is fleshed out with attention to practical details. The Talmudic corpus painstakingly defines and distinguishes prohibitions and obligations at law, and addresses straightforward questions of legal procedure, including rules of contracts, agency, property, and the like.

These three structural lines—sources of authority, ethical and theological balance, practical needs of legal procedure—express the Talmud's own view of its goals and aims. But the upshot for our purposes is that rabbinic reflection upon a given part of the Decalogue (or upon any other biblical regulation) will be complex and full of apparently conflicting impulses. This sticky web of reasoning leads Jewish law, as I shall argue in chapters 4 and 5 of this volume, to its casuistic orientation. Abstract rules—even the Ten Utterances if unaccompanied by rabbinic explanation—often miss the mark, for the halakhic web can only be instantiated through consideration of a particular case.

4. In Search of the Rabbinic Meaning of Scripture

The rabbinic approach to the Ten Commandments entails moving beyond Scripture's plain meanings. As the rabbis constructed the web of law central to their interpretation of the Ten Utterances, what did they tell us in detail? What meaning did they impute to these verses or to the abstract Commandments they represent? For the most part, the Talmud's authors' attitude toward Scripture may be summed up as follows: rabbinic teaching constitutes the Oral Law, the lens through which one must read the Written Torah. If the Talmudic units discussed thus far show that people must coordinate the two aspects of Torah, in the materials that follow we shall again see the concept of Torah at the heart of rabbinic interpretation.

In Judaic theology, Torah has a broader meaning than an initial reference to a biblical rule ("This is the law (*Torah*) of the communion-meal sacrifice" [Lev. 7:11]) or even the wider application of the term to the whole of Pentateuchal law (as in the appellation *Tanakh*, an acronym for *Torah* [Pentateuch], *Nᵊviim* [Prophets], and *Kᵊtuvim* [Writings]).

For the rabbis, all of God's revelation, hence the entire Bible, plus all rabbinic law, interpretation, history, and lore that might accompany it, constitutes Torah. Torah defines and limns all Judaic movements, and represents the major focus of the rabbinic worldview. In their study of the Ten Utterances, the rabbis take the opportunity to make major statements of Torah-centered theology, in particular addressing the study of Torah, the power of Torah, and the history of Torah.

Idolatry and the Study of Torah

The Ten Commandments open somewhat strangely, without issuing an explicit ordinance or injunction. "I the LORD am your God . . . " neither proscribes nor prescribes any action; the opening Utterance rather serves as a prologue that establishes the historical relationship between God and the Jewish people: " . . . who brought you out of the land of Egypt, the house of bondage." This statement of God's action in behalf of the Israelite nation sets the way for a covenantal imperative: as God has acted to rescue and redeem the Israelites, so they must act in accord with God's commands as specified in the remaining Utterances. To act in any other manner would be to disregard God's sovereignty.

The Second Utterance, "You shall have no other gods besides Me. . . . You shall not bow down to them or serve them," forms the counterpart to this prologue. Jews show their understanding of their particular relationship with God through their own actions, first and foremost, through worshipping God alone. Taken together, the first two Utterances thus demand the crucial and absolute monotheism characteristic of biblical and later Judaism.

So between the historical relationship of God toward the Israelites and the prohibition against worshipping other gods is found a program of action for every Jew. The life of holiness (*qedushah*) is attained by obeying the law given by the Redeemer from Egyptian slavery. For the rabbis, this law was found in the remaining eight Utterances as well as in the whole Torah. Any violation of Torah, therefore, constituted an act of idolatry; conversely, the law against idolatry implied the entire active *halakhah*.

The Talmudic materials we shall now survey build to this correlation between idolatry and violation of the remaining Utterances. We begin with the rabbis' statement of the seriousness with which they regarded monotheistic belief and practice, expressed in a simple equation of a statement of allegiance to an idol with actual worship of that idol. This emphasis on one's statements, even in the absence of more explicit deeds such as bowing down before the image, constitutes a deviation from normal legal procedure, which takes into account accomplished deeds, but requires explicit confirmation of the meaning of a person's speech.[1] In the following unit of the Talmud, formally an explanation of a passage from the Mishnah, even one's words and intentions may suffice to convict one of the serious sin of idolatrous worship.

Mishnah Sanhedrin 7:6

"[These felons are put to death through stoning:] . . . *One who worships an idol"* (M. San. 7:4)—All the same is one who worships, one who actually sacrifices, one who offers incense, one who pours a libation, one who bows down, and one who accepts it as a god, saying, "You are my god."

But one who hugs it, kisses it, sweeps before it, sprinkles before it, washes it, anoints it, puts clothing on it, and puts shoes on it, [merely] transgresses a negative commandment (Exod. 20:5).

One who vows by its name or one who fulfills a vow made in its name [merely] transgresses a negative commandment (Exod. 23:13).

One who uncovers himself to Baal Peor [is stoned, for] this is how one worships it. One who tosses a pebble at Merkolis [i.e., Hermes, is stoned, for] this is how one worships it.

Yerushalmi Sanhedrin 7:9 [Venice: 28b; Vilna: 37a–38a]

How might we derive Scripture's warning against worshipping an idol? *"[You shall not make for yourself a sculptured image* . . . *]; you shall not bow down to them or serve them"* (Exod. 20:4–5).

How might we derive that the penalty is extirpation? *"[But the person, be he citizen or stranger, who acts deceitfully] reviles the LORD; that person shall be cut off from among his people"* (Num. 15:30). But doesn't that

---

1. See Louis Jacobs, *The Talmudic Argument: A Study in Talmudic Reasoning and Methodology* (Cambridge: Cambridge University Press, 1984), pp. 101–9, on the irrelevance of mental reservations to the validity of contracts.

verse refer to one who blasphemes, [and not to an idol worshipper]? [Those who would wipe out God's name through blasphemy and idolators are equivalent to one another], like one person who says to another, "You have wiped the plate clean and left nothing on it," [likewise a blasphemer leaves nothing to worship but idols]. R. Simeon b. Eleazar stated this in a parable: "The matter is comparable to two people sitting with a plate of beans between them. One of them stuck out his hand and wiped the whole plate clean and left nothing on it. So a blasphemer or an idolator leaves not a single religious duty after him."

How might we derive a [court-administered] punishment? *"[If there is found among you . . . a man or woman . . . who has turned to the worship of other gods and bowed down to them . . .], you shall take the man or woman who did that wicked thing out to the public place, and you shall stone them, man or woman, to death"* (Deut. 17:2–5).

"You shall not . . . serve them . . . " (Exod. 20:5)—[given the wording of this verse, which refers to *them,*] I might have thought that one has transgressed only after serving all the idols in the world. But Torah teaches, *"You shall not bow down to them"* (Exod. 20:5). "Bowing down" was part of the general rule against [worshipping idols], so why was it explicitly singled out? This allows us to draw an analogy: Just as bowing down is distinctive because it is a single action [before one idol at a time], and people are liable for that action alone, so I assert that for every individual deed, people are liable for a single action [before a single idol].

Even though R. Simeon b. Eleazar has said, "[If] one sacrificed, offered incense, and poured a libation in a single spell of inadvertence, he is liable on only one count," he concedes that if one has worshipped an idol in the correct way in which it is worshipped, or in the way in which the Most High is worshipped, or through an act of worshipful prostration, he is liable on each count [this is because Scripture specifies worship and prostration as distinct, forbidden acts, so each is culpable by itself]. . . .

. . . How might we derive from Scripture that [a person is culpable merely] for saying, "You are my god"? Rav Avun in the name of the rabbis from over [in Babylonia]: *"[They have made themselves a molten calf] and bowed low to it and sacrificed to it, saying, 'This is your god, O Israel, [who brought you out of the land of Egypt!]'"* (Exod. 32:8).

On that basis, one should not be culpable unless he [performs all three actions]: he must bow down and sacrifice to the idol,[2] as well as making the prohibited statement.

Said R. Yose, "[In mentioning sacrificing and bowing down] Scripture's intent was merely to record the extent of Israel's degradation: 'They have bowed low to it'—not to the Most High. 'They have sacrificed to it'—not to the Most High. 'Saying to it, [this is your god, O Israel] . . .' —not the Most High.

In the end, how do [we prove that this verse indicates that one is culpable for merely saying, "You are my god," without a confirming deed]? Here an act of speech is mentioned, and an act of speech is mentioned in the case of the one who incites people to idolatry. Just as an act of speech stated with reference to one who incites people to idolatry is treated as a concrete deed [and so implies culpability], so an act of speech noted here likewise is treated as a concrete deed [and implies culpability]. . . .

. . . R. Samuel bar Naḥmani in the name of R. Hoshaiah: "One who says to an idol, 'You are my god,' brings up a dispute between Rabbi and sages, [who disagree as to whether the statement does in fact constitute a deed and so implies culpability.]"

But if one bows down to it, what is the law? R. Yoḥanan said, "All concur that one who bends at the waist is liable, [for we have a concrete deed.]" [By the same logic, shouldn't merely saying something also constitute a deed], for what difference is there between raising and lowering one's body and raising and lowering one's lips?

R. Yoḥanan said, "The analogy is subject to a dispute." Resh Laqish said, "The dispute [concerns whether merely bending at the waist itself is a culpable deed]." Said R. Zeira, "The following verse of Scripture supports the view of Resh Laqish: 'For the citizen among the Israelites and for the stranger who resides among them—you shall have one protocol (Torah)[3] for anyone who acts in error' (Num. 15:29). [This indicates that we require a concrete act, and bending at the waist does not suffice.] I thus derive that a concrete deed is culpable. But hugging and bowing down, which are not concrete deeds—whence shall we derive proof?"[4]

---

2. Printed editions read: "he must sacrifice and offer incense to the idol."
3. Jewish Publication Society, *TANAKH*: "ritual."
4. For parallel passages, see B. Keritot 7a–b, B. Zevaḥim 106a–b, B. Ḥullin 66a–b, and B. Sanhedrin 65a–b.

As a whole, the passage just presented implies that making a graven image merely constitutes a violation of a negative commandment,[5] surely a crime, but roughly equivalent to a misdemeanor. The more serious, felonious offense is committed by someone who worships the idol. These two issues emerge here because of their proximity within the Second Utterance: one must not take another god, by worshipping and bowing down to an idol (Exod. 20:3); and one must not make a graven image of that god (Exod. 20:4).

But the deeper meaning of this pericope is established in a systematic and gradually unfolding manner. After citing the relevant Mishnaic prohibitions, the Talmud opens by indicating its scriptural sources. By directly invoking the Ten Commandments and other verses nearby, the rabbis established scriptural warrant both for prohibitions and for punishments attending idolatry and idol making.

The Talmud next moves on to arguments that establish a special set of rules regarding idol worship. The Talmud often asks whether a person who committed many transgressions within a single fit of sinful conduct ought to be liable on but one count, for the one set of actions. In general, the answer depends upon the severity of the offenses involved. For its part, idol worship constitutes so serious an offense that a stringent standard applies, especially when one worships the graven image as if it were the one true God, by bowing down or sacrificing to it. Accordingly, to underscore the extreme nature of the transgression, each act is taken disjunctively: each constitutes a separate and individual charge of worshipping an idol, with its individual penalty or punishment.

Finally, the matter extends to the logical extreme. Even those who merely state that they have taken another god are deemed culpable for worshipping an idol. The act of stating one's alle-

---

5. See Neusner, *The Talmud of the Land of Israel, vol. 31, Tractate Sanhedrin*, pp. 236–42.

giance to an idol carries with it the same set of consequences and punishments as more concrete acts of worship toward the false god.

This importance of one's words within the Talmudic materials shows the scribal concerns of the rabbis: as guardians of the Torah—here the Word of and about God—they tolerate no abuse of language. At the core of their system, the rabbis take the Second Utterance to be more than a simple prohibition: words themselves constitute actions to be regulated under the rubric of avoiding idolatry.

In expressing its stringency in regard to idol worship, the foregoing passage utilizes a common rhetorical technique, referred to as "general and specific," which will be found also in the upcoming Talmudic unit. As we saw, this structure involves a general biblical rule—"You shall not worship them"—followed by a particular instance of that rule—"You must not bow down to them." Rabbinic hermeneutics, summarized in the famous Thirteen Exegetical Principles of Rabbi Ishmael, require that the general rule be limited by the specific statement.

Beraita de-Rabbi Ishmael (Prologue to Sifra)

Rabbi Ishmael says, "By thirteen methods the Torah has been interpreted. . . . "

. . . 6. By means of a general statement and a specific statement. How does this work? [In Lev. 1:2, "When any of you presents an offering] of cattle" is the general statement; "from the herd or from the flock" is the specific statement. [When you have] a general statement and a specific statement, the general statement includes only [that implied by] the specific statement.[6]

Such summaries of rabbinic exegetical principles do not prescribe proper interpretive technique for the neophyte, but rath-

---

6. Translated by Gary Porton, in Jacob Neusner, *Sifra: An Analytic Translation*, 3 vols., Brown Judaic Studies 138, 139, and 140 (Atlanta, Ga.: Scholars Press, 1988), vol. 1, pp. 57–59.

er are inductive, generated after the fact by examination of rhetorical patterns found in Talmudic and Midrashic literature. Nonetheless, they do draw our attention to a central theme in the rabbinic corpus broadly, and in the treatment of the Ten Commandments in particular: the manner in which Scripture deals with various rules, including broad principles and more specific instances, is to be taken with great seriousness.

The following pericope continues this thoroughly attentive attitude toward Scripture. The issue here is familiar from the foregoing units: based on exegesis of Scripture, can we establish that multiple counts of idolatry committed in a single act of sin carry multiple punishments? While the main point of the unit is to clarify the fine points of the "general and specific" hermeneutic, we need at the outset to note the comparison established between the Fourth Commandment—Sabbath observance—and the Second—"You shall have no other gods besides Me." Such comparisons of a particular Commandment and the Decalogue's prohibition against idolatry will become a common theme in the materials that follow. For the rabbis, any transgression of the Ten Utterances implied a denial of God's omniscience and omnipotence, and thus constituted an idolatrous act.

Yerushalmi Nazir 6:1 [Venice: 54c; Vilna 24b]

Rav Zakkai taught before R. Yohanan: "If one has sacrificed, burned incense, and poured a libation [to an idol] in a single spell of inadvertence, one is liable on each count [and not simply for the general charge of idol worship]."

Said to him R. Yohanan, "O Babylonian! You have forded three rivers [on your way to the Land of Israel, and in your exhaustion] you have forgotten [the proper rule]: He is liable on only a single count."

[A more nuanced version of the rule follows]: Up to the moment one breaks the idol into pieces [and so still fails to recognize he is forbidden to worship the idol], he is liable on a single count, but not on multiple counts [for the one fit of inadvertence]. But once he breaks the idol into pieces, [indicating that he now knows he is transgressing,] he is liable on multiple counts, and not solely on a single count!

R. Ba bar Mamel inquired of R. Zeira: "Shouldn't he be liable on each count, [that is, for each individual action in connection with idolatry], just as is true with regard to the Sabbath? [Scripture states:] '*[But the seventh day is a Sabbath of the* LORD *your God;] you shall not do any work*' (Exod. 20:10)—this represents a generalization; '*You shall kindle no fire throughout your settlements [on the Sabbath day]*' (Exod. 35:3)—this represents a specific detail. Now was not the prohibition against kindling fire part of the generalization? It was singled out to teach you that, just as kindling a fire is an individual action, for which people are independently liable, so each act [violating the Sabbath] independently imposes culpability.

"Now here too [in the case of idolatry, we may argue along these same lines]: '*You shall not serve them*' (Exod. 20:5)—this represents a generalization; '*You shall not bow down to them*' (Exod. 20:5)—this represents a specific detail. Now was not the prohibition against bowing down part of the generalization? It was singled out to teach you that just as bowing down is the action of individuals [before a single idol at a time], for which people are independently liable, so each act [of idol worship] independently imposes culpability."

[R. Zeira said]:"One may reply to you [that the comparisons really are dissimilar]. In the case of the Sabbath, the general rule is stated in one place, and the specific details are stated in another context entirely. In the case of idolatry, by contrast, the general rule is side by side with the specific details."

[R. Ba bar Mamel] said to him, "Isn't it written, '*You must not worship any other god, [because the* LORD, *whose name is Impassioned, is an impassioned God]*' (Exod: 34:14). [Taking that verse into account], you have a general rule stated in one place, and the specific details stated in another context. [The analogy to Sabbath law should hold.]"

[R. Zeira] said to him, "Since you do not interpret in line with the verse that stands by its side, you also may not interpret on the basis of a verse that is located in some other place."

Associates say, "It makes no difference whatsoever whether the generalization is in one place and the specific details are in some other context, or whether the general rule and the specific details are in the same place. [The analogy doesn't hold up fully because] in the case of the Sabbath, we have a general rule and afterward specific details. But in the case of idolatry, you have the specific details first, and then the general rule."

R. Yose says, "It makes no difference whatsoever whether you have a general rule and afterward specific details, or whether you have specific details first and only afterward a general rule. In any event, it adds up to a general rule and a specific exemplification thereof. But [still the analogy between Sabbath and idol worship doesn't hold up.] [For in reference to] the Sabbath, you have a general rule dealing with Sabbath work and a specific exemplification also dealing with Sabbath work. In the case of idolatry, by contrast, the general rule deals with idolatrous acts, while the specific details deal with acts of worship [carried out not only toward idols, but also toward] the Most High."
. . . [7]

On the surface, the rabbis bring no particular, unique agenda to this exercise, for which the Bible alone supplies the topic. But that is ripe with meaning. The rabbis maintain above all a vital interest in the meaning and workings of Scripture itself. The specification of appropriate punishments for multiple acts of idolatry serves only as a logical extension of the Hebrew Bible's rules, and the solution further emphasizes the scriptural outlook of the rabbis by invoking (and working through the possibilities of) the Sabbath law analogy.

But the comparison and contrast between the command, "The seventh day is a Sabbath to the LORD your God: you shall not do any work" (Exod. 20:10) and the prohibition against idolatry loom large. These two Utterances are woven together at a deep level, in both style and meaning. The "general and specific" hermeneutic is applied evenly to both commandments, linking them structurally and rhetorically. And although the analogy is repeatedly tried and rejected, the upshot is that a single set of actions can involve multiple violations of either law, establishing a substantive analogy between one of the Ten Utterances and the absolute prohibition against idol worship.

This pattern of tying a particular Commandment back to the anti-idolatrous Second Utterance is, in my view, no accident.

---

7. For parallel passages, see B. Sanhedrin 62a–b and B. Shabbat 70a–b.

When the rabbis delve most deeply into study of Torah and of the Ten Commandments, they wish to highlight the paramount nature of monotheistic law and action, usually by precisely the type of comparison established here.

A further instance of this identity between the Ten Commandments and the prohibition against idolatrous behavior is found in Talmudic discussion of perjury. The discourse on perjury occurs in a passage regarding appropriate punishments for the crime of rape. As we shall see, the sage Nathan bar Hoshaiah establishes that, in certain cases, rapists must pay monetary compensation to their victims, but are not to be flogged for their crime. This perspective, that payment of actual damages might obviate the need for a court-imposed punishment, sets the stage for R. Simeon b. Laqish's opinion regarding perjury, which he deems punishable by both flogging *and* imposition of a fine. Toward the end of the passage, the analogy is taken a step further, so that perjury is deemed tantamount to cultic sacrilege. The point of the unit as a whole, then, is to equate perjury or bearing false witness to other principal types of improper behavior—whether sexual (i.e., committing rape) or idolatrous (i.e., through committing cultic sacrilege).

Mishnah Ketuvot 3:1

[In] these [cases, although the] girls [involved are invalid for marriage to an Israelite], they [nonetheless] receive a fine [from a man who seduces them]:

He who has sexual relations with a Mamzer girl, a Netin girl, or a Samaritan girl; he who has sexual relations with a convert girl, with a slave girl, or with a girl taken captive, [if the girl] was redeemed, converted, or was freed before the age of three years and one day [and who therefore remains in the status of virgins]; he who has sexual relations with his sister, with the sister of his father, with the sister of his mother, with his wife's sister, with the wife of his brother, with the wife of the brother of his father, or with a menstruating woman—they receive a fine [from the man who seduces them].

Even though [one who has sexual relations with] them is subject to extirpation, one does not incur through them the death penalty at the hands of an earthly court.

Yerushalmi Ketuvot 3:1 [Venice: 27b; Vilna: 16b–17a]

Nathan bar Hoshaiah said, "[There is an apparent conflict between the present rule, that a girl receives a financial penalty paid by a rapist, who is not flogged, and M. Mak. 3:1, which specifies that the penalty for rape is flogging.] [This apparent contradiction may be resolved by noting that] here we deal with a young girl, while there we deal with a grown woman: a young girl receives a financial penalty, but no flogging [is incurred by one who has sexual relations with her]. [Rape of] a woman incurs a flogging, but she does not receive a financial penalty."

But doesn't [a grown woman] receive compensation for shame or personal injury? [A grown woman therefore receives both monetary compensation and the pleasure of seeing the perpetrator flogged. Even though a young girl receives a fine in place of the flogging, shouldn't she also receive monetary compensation for shame and injury?]

The rabbis of Caesarea say, "Interpret the current rule to speak of a case in which the man seduced the girl [so there is no question of shame or personal injury]; or to one in which the girl forgave him [these forms of compensation and did not exact payment of them.] [Accordingly, there is no incongruity in the penalties specified here and at M. Mak. 3:1]."

[In any case,] Nathan bar Hoshaiah must maintain that in a case involving both a flogging and monetary compensation, one pays the monetary penalty and is not flogged.

But why should the man not be flogged and also pay? [Scripture says,] "*As his guilt warrants*" (Deut. 25:2) so you hold him guilty for a single offense [and so a single punishment]; but you do not hold him guilty for two offenses.

Perhaps we should let him pay and not suffer a flogging, as in the case of perjured witnesses. Just as you say in that other context of perjured witnesses that they pay and are not flogged, here, too, he should pay and not be flogged.

Said R. Jonah, "The reason behind the position of Nathan bar Hoshaiah is [simpler]: "*As his guilt warrants*" refers to one who, through being flogged, suffers a just penalty for his offense. This then excludes anyone to whom the sages say, 'Go and pay a monetary penalty.'"

The following statement of the Mishnah differs from R. Simeon b. Laqish: *He who deliberately eats produce in the status of heave offering pays the principal but does not pay the added fifth* (M. Ter. 7:1).

Now from the viewpoint of Nathan bar Hoshaiah, who said that if he pays [actual damages, he then incurs no further punishment, as above in the case of a rapist], there are no problems. As to the view of R. Yoḥanan, who said that if one was warned beforehand, he is flogged, but if he was not warned, he [merely] pays [the damages], one may interpret the case to be one in which one did the deed deliberately but without an advance warning.

But in the view of R. Simeon b. Laqish, there is no difference whether or not one did the deed inadvertently or deliberately, whether one was warned or was not. . . .

. . . R. Simeon b. Laqish is consistent with his position enunciated elsewhere:

"All were subject to the general statement, '*You shall not bear false witness against your neighbor*' (Exod. 20:16). The perjured witness then was treated as a special case: '*And you shall do to him as he had conspired to do*' (Deut. 19:19). Is that not so that he should pay monetary compensation?

"Now here, too, all were subject to the general statement, '*An outsider shall not eat of a holy thing*' (Lev. 22:10). Then a special case was expressed as follows: '*And when a man inadvertently eats what was holy . . .* ' (Lev. 22:14), indicating that he pays compensation. [So even though all others who are flogged for sins committed inadvertently are exempt from having to pay monetary penalties, in this case one is liable.]"

Now has it not been taught [that there is no difference of opinion in this particular matter, for] sages concur with R. Meir in the case of one who steals heave offering belonging to his fellow and who ate it, that he is flogged and he also pays monetary compensation? [Even in a case of a deliberate sin, therefore, one may be flogged and also pay monetary compensation.]

[But that is a special case,] for one who eats prohibited fat belonging to himself is flogged. [The case is different, since the monetary compensation owing to the fellow is quite separate from the flogging owing to heaven.][8]

Throughout this set of analogies and comparisons, two paramount rabbinic interests control the discussion, namely, appropriate sexuality and proper Temple practice. Perjury therefore is first equated to sexual immorality (rape), and then equated to sacrilege in cultic procedures (an Israelite's eating consecrated heave offering).

The issue of idolatry lurks just behind the scenes. Bearing false witness in the end is compared to violation of proper Temple process regarding the substance of a sacrifice or offering. Such improper offerings may be described as foreign, as for example, when Aaron's sons offered alien incense to God (see Lev. 10:1–3). In other words, sacrilege in the Temple simply forms the other side of the coin of idolatrous worship: the latter involves sacrificing to the wrong god, the former involves making the wrong sacrifice to God.

Can we now move, like the Rabbis, from the specific to the general, and so bring to full exposition the rabbinic equation between violation of the Ten Commandments and idolatrous practice? The Fourth Commandment, Sabbath observance, is specific; the Ninth Commandment, against false witness, is specific; even the Commandment prohibiting idolatry or improper cultic procedure is specific. But for the rabbis, only the study of Torah is truly a general and absolute obligation. At the outset of Tractate Peah, we find this value judgment clearly stated.

Mishnah Peah 1:1

These are things the benefits of which a person enjoys in this world, while the principal remains for the world-to-come: (1) [deeds done in] honor of father and mother, (2) [performance of] righteous deeds, and

---

8. For a parallel passage, see B. Yevamot 90a–b.

(3) acts that bring about peace between one person and another. But (4) study of Torah is equal to all of them together.

The mention of honoring one's parents, the Fifth Commandment, is largely beside the point. Rather, the enthronement of Torah study as the meritorious activity par excellence reveals a crucial belief of the rabbinic thinkers: proper human behavior is subsumed under a single broad heading, namely, study of God's revelation. So long as one's focus remains upon God's message, the student remains enraptured by God alone—and could not possibly deviate from monotheistic belief, either in thought (through idolatrous worship or declaration) or deed (through transgression of any of God's law).

The next segment of text fully establishes the rabbinic agenda regarding Torah study as opposed to transgression, and also undergirds the connection between idolatrous belief and sinful action. The flow of argument follows this path: in defining idolatry, the rabbis claim that the gentile soothsayer Balaam (see Num. 23) will have no part in the world to come because of information he supplied to Balak, king of the Midianites, when the latter tried to defeat the Israelites. Balaam, by suggesting that the Midianites could ensnare the Israelites in sexual improprieties, provided a means for Balak's victory: God himself would punish the Israelites for sexual misconduct. This mention of sexual immorality draws in its wake a consideration of the idol Baal Peor, whom one worships by exposing oneself.

Mishnah Sanhedrin 10:2

Three kings and four ordinary folk have no portion in the world to come.

Three kings: Ahab, Jeroboam, and Manasseh. R. Judah says, "Manasseh has a portion in the world to come, since it is said, 'He prayed to [God] and [God] granted his prayer, heard his plea, and returned him to Jerusalem to his kingdom' (2 Chron. 33:13)." They said to [R. Judah], "[God] brought him back to his kingdom, but not to the world to come."

Four ordinary folk: Balaam, Doeg, Ahitophel, and Gahazi.

Yerushalmi Sanhedrin 10:2 [Venice: 28d; Vilna: 51b-52a]

Now what did the evil Balaam do [to warrant losing his portion in the world to come]? He gave advice to Balak son of Zippor on how to cause Israel's downfall by the sword:

He said to him, "The God of this nation hates fornication. So put up your daughters for fornication, and you will rule over them." [Balak] replied, "And will [the Moabites] listen to me [when I tell them to turn their daughters into whores]?" [Balaam] said to him, "Put up your own daughter first; when they see that, they will do as you tell them." That is in line with the following verse of Scripture: *"[The name of the Midianite woman who was killed was Cozbi daughter of Zur]; he was the tribal head of an ancestral house in Midian"* (Num. 25:15).

What did [Balak's followers] do [to enact this plan]? They built temples from Beth Ha-Yeshimmon to Snow Mountain, and they set in them women selling various kinds of sweets. They put an older lady outside, and a young girl inside. When the Israelites were eating and drinking, one of them would go for a stroll through the marketplace, and he would buy something from a stallkeeper. The older lady would sell him the thing for whatever it was worth, but the young girl would say, "Come on in and get it for less." So it was on the first day, the second day, and the third day. And then, [the young temptress] would say to him, "From now on, you're one of us. Come in and choose whatever you like."

When [the Israelite] went in, there was a flagon full of wine, strong Ammonite wine, which serves as an aphrodisiac, with an enticing scent.—Now up to this time the wine of gentiles had not been prohibited for Israelite use by reason of its being libation wine.—Next [the girl] would say to him, "Do you want to drink a cup of wine," and if he replied, "Yes," she gave him a cup of wine. When he drank it, the wine would burn in him like snake venom. Then he would say to her, "Surrender yourself to me." She would say to him, "Do you want me to 'surrender' myself to you?" If he replied, "Yes," she took out an image of Peor from her bosom, and she said to him, "Bow down to this, and I'll surrender myself to you."

He would say to her, "Do you think I am going to bow down to an idol?" And she would say to him, "You don't really bow down to it, you just expose yourself to it." This is in line with that which sages have said, *"One who exposes himself to Baal Peor—this is the appropriate manner of worshipping it; and he who tosses a stone at Merkolis—this is the appropriate manner of worshipping it"* (M. San. 7:6).

. . . Then she would say to him, "Separate yourself from the Torah of Moses, and I shall 'surrender' myself to you." That is in line with the following verse of Scripture: *"[I found Israel as pleasing as grapes in the wilderness; your fathers seemed to Me like the first fig to ripen on a fig tree.] But when they came to Baal Peor, they turned aside to shamefulness; then they became as detested as they had been loved"* (Hos. 9:10)—they became detestable to their Father who is in Heaven.

Said R. Eleazar, "Just as one cannot pull this nail from the door without taking along a piece of wood, so it is not possible to separate from Peor without [the loss of] souls."

Once Subetah from Ulam hired out his ass to a gentile woman, [and was leading her upon the ass to take her] to bow down to Peor. When they got to the House of Peor, she said to him, "Wait for me here, while I go in and worship Peor." When she came out, he said to her, "Wait for me here, until I go in and do just what you did." What did he do? [Hoping to desecrate the idol], he went in, defecated, and wiped himself on the nose of Peor. But everyone present praised him, and said to him, "Nobody does it better!!"[9]

Idolatry clearly was of paramount interest to the rabbis, being the one exegetical point that unites the various passages presented in this section. The rabbis widely discussed this transgression and accorded it the most severe gravity. We have seen the general topic in diverse rhetorical settings, aimed at spelling out details of rabbinic hermeneutics. And the individual Commandments mentioned in those varied contexts—Sabbath observance, bearing false witness, honoring parents—all are invoked in direct connection to the prohibition against idolatry.

The rabbis' basic assertion about idolatry, the foundational prohibition contained within the Ten Utterances, is revealed plainly by the enticing idolatress. Her two parallel lemmas spell out the full meaning of the Baal Peor story: "Bow down to Baal

---

9. For a parallel passage, see B. Sanhedrin 106a.

Peor and I'll surrender myself to you. . . . " "Separate yourself from the Torah of Moses and I'll surrender myself to you. . . . " These suggestive propositions make explicit the equation of idolatry with all other types of transgression, as opposed to study of Torah, which includes every meritorious activity. Here we have the first major message of rabbinism: idolatry and study of Torah exist in inverse relation to one another. Nothing is worse than idolatry, because idolatry is the denial of Torah; nothing is better than study of Torah, for this alone leads to the life of holiness. The rabbis adjure the Talmudic student: don't cease study of Torah, God's own revelation, for to do so would be to ignore God's special relationship to the people of Israel, as found in the First Utterance. Moreover, cessation of the life of Torah would constitute the most direct transgression of the Ten Utterances possible.

Miracles and the Power of Torah

In the previous units, we saw how rabbinic discourses, while clearly linked to particular Commandments, nonetheless reached the somewhat surprising identity between idolatry, transgression in general, and even momentary cessation of Torah study or separation from the life of Torah. By reading each of the Utterances in light of the covenantal relationship established between God's redeeming Israel and Israel's worship of God alone, the rabbis assigned ever richer meaning to the biblical Decalogue.

In this section, I present two Talmudic discourses from tractate Sanhedrin that evince the creative power of the rabbis' approach toward the biblical materials. Here, the Utterances serve as a starting block for rabbinic discourse, and formally, the discussion will focus on a given commandment. But the rabbis' interests and assertions nevertheless come through quite clearly. When they have the floor and feel rather unconstrained, what do the rabbis say in connection with the Ten Commandments? They claim that miracles result from the power inherent in knowledge of Torah.

The first passage I present addresses (at least nominally) the Ninth Commandment, against bearing false witness. The main point, fully consonant with earlier biblical notions of retribution, is that false witnesses ought to receive the same punishment or means of execution as would someone convicted of the crime about which the perjurer testified. This point is occasioned by the Mishnah's conflation of three apparently separate categories: those who prophesy in the name of an idol, those who have sexual relations with married women, and those who bear false witness against a priest's daughter.

Mishnah Sanhedrin 11:6

"[These individuals receive the death penalty through strangulation:] One who prophesies in the name of an idol . . . " (cf. M. San. 11:1)—

If he says, "This is what the idol told me," then even if he correctly stated the law, declaring unclean that which in fact is unclean, and declaring clean that which in fact is clean, [still he is to be executed by strangulation].

" . . . One who has sexual relations with a married woman . . . " (cf. M. San. 11:1)—

From the moment she enters the domain of the husband in marriage, even if she has not yet had sexual relations with him, [another man] who has sexual relations with her is put to death by strangling.

" . . . And those who bear false witness against the priest's daughter and against one who has sexual relations with her" (cf. M. San. 11:1)—

For all those who bear false witness suffer that same mode of execution, except for those who bear false witness against the priest's daughter and her lover, [who normally would be stoned or burned to death].

Yerushalmi Sanhedrin 11:6 [Venice: 30c; Vilna: 57a-b]

Said R. Yose b. Ḥaninah, "All [types of false prophecy] are governed by the general rule [of the Ninth Commandment], *'You shall not bear false witness against your neighbor'* (Exod. 20:13). Yet *'One who prophesies in the name of an idol . . . '* (M. San. 11:1) was singled out so as to teach that, whether he gave a sign or worked a miracle, whether [the prophecy] directly concerned idolatry or merely the other commandments [the prophecy should be ignored and the idol prophet executed by strangulation]. . . . "

. . . As to two prophets who prophesied simultaneously, or two prophets who prophesied in the same town—

R. Isaac and R. Hoshaiah disputed: one said, "Each must give a sign or work a miracle; [whichever does so is the true prophet]." But the other stated, "Neither is required to give a sign or work a miracle."

The former, who said that he must produce a sign or miracle, objected to the latter, who required no such evidence, "Is it not written, *'Hezekiah asked Isaiah, "What is the sign that the LORD will heal me, and that I shall go up to the House of the LORD on the third day?"'* (2 Kings 20:8)."

The latter replied, "That is a special case. [A sign was required] because they dealt with the resurrection of the dead: *'In two days [God] will make us whole again; on the third day [God] will raise us up, and we shall be whole by [God's] favor'* (Hos. 6:2)."[10]

Two points require explicit comment. Notice first how the prohibition against perjury finds its fullest explication in the context of idolatrous practice, here, prophecy in an idol's name. As above, the rabbis (first in the Mishnah, followed by those of the Talmud) explicitly introduced the prohibition against idolatry, even when a plain reading of the biblical verse seems to have had nothing to do with that theme. Here, the Talmud asserts the absolute unreliability of idolatrous prophecy, for this is tantamount to bearing false witness about the idol's ability as an oracle or true divinity. Such messages from mere wood or stone obviously are to be utterly rejected, even when the law is stated correctly, even when the prophecy is accompanied by a sign or wonder. In so ruling, the rabbis once again highlight the central place occupied by the prohibition against idolatrous practice.

But a second point emerges from the tenor of the Talmud's discussion. At issue here is not merely the link between the

---

10. For parallel passages, see B. Makkot 2a and B. Sanhedrin 90a–b.

transgressions of adultery, perjury, and idolatry. Rather, we have an examination of the potential conflict between false prophecy, on the one hand, and true prophecy in the name of the Torah, on the other. In a case of conflicting prophecy, how would the rabbis determine the true prophet? They assume that a true prophet will have the full backing of the Divine voice, and so will be able to work miracles and produce signs of authority.[11] This development in the Talmudic materials is characteristic of the rabbis, who here use the occasion of discussing the Ten Commandments to speak of the power of Torah and its ability to work wonders.

A complementary passage, from Yerushalmi Sanhedrin 10:2, forms the basis of the remainder of this section, and presents us with an interesting shift in topic. Having discussed three categories of perjurers, we now turn our attention to the polar opposite of these transgressors, to three sages, people learned in Torah. And just as the Talmud specified miraculous behaviors and the executions appropriate for perjury, so, too, it lists wonders worked by the Torah sages, as well as miraculous punishments they brought upon others or themselves. The two essays thus provide a balanced discourse—three sinners, their miracles and punishments; three sages, their miracles and judgments.

The three somewhat lengthy "sage" segments involve biblical characters, claimed to be "powerful in Torah." The first of these is Phineas (see Num. 25:6–9), who performed six miracles and magically defeated the idol-prophet Balaam. The second sage presented is Doeg the Edomite (see 1 Sam. 22:9–23), who, for the crime of slaughtering many of God's priests, was executed by a miraculous fire, despite his advanced learning. Third and finally, the Talmud recounts stories of Ahitophel (see 2 Sam. 16–17), whose knowledge of Torah gave him greater supernat-

---

11. See Neusner, *Judaism in Society*, pp. 174–77, for explanation of the rabbis' supernatural authority, which issues in miraculous abilities.

ural powers than the Israelite King, yet who submitted to the divine hegemony of the Davidic dynasty.

It is worth noting that explicit mention of the Ten Commandments occurs only toward the end, in the story about King David and Aḥitophel. Specifically, David, in danger of losing his life in a flood, forces the Torah sage Aḥitophel (with whom he had been feuding) to halt the waters miraculously, which had been stopped up since the revelation of the Ten Utterances at Sinai. And part of the feud between Aḥitophel and King David had to do with the special qualities of the Ark of the Covenant, which contained the shards of the Stone Tablets.

So the Ten Utterances here serve as an historical landmark, as a detail of passing, background information. The larger goal of this Talmudic passage, by contrast, is to point up the true nature of Torah's power. A person with knowledge of God's revelation is capable of miraculous behavior, no matter what his or her character, good or bad. Making this point in connection with the Ten Commandments (recall that Y. San. 10:2 earlier discussed the idolatrous worship of Baal Peor) demonstrates that the Utterances, for the rabbis, were part of the broader scheme of the Torah.

Yerushalmi Sanhedrin 10:2 [Venice: 28d–29b; Vilna: 52a-b]

"Just then one of the Israelites came and brought a Midianite woman over to his companions, in the sight of Moses [and of the whole Israelite community who were weeping at the entrance of the Tent of Meeting]" (Num. 25:6)— what is the meaning of, *"In the sight of Moses"*? It was as if the man said, "Here's mud in your eye, Moses!"

[The man who had taken the Midianite woman] said [to Moses], "Is your Zipporah not Midianite, and haven't you treated her as if her feet were cloven? [Isn't she 'kosher,' fit to be your wife?] Your woman is clean but my woman is not?!"

Now Phineas was there. He said, "Is there no man here who will kill him even at the expense of his life?" . . . As soon as he saw that no Israelite was about to do anything, Phineas stood up from his Sanhedrin seat, took a spear, and put the iron tip under his belt. He began to lean upon the shaft [of the spear, as if using a cane] all the way to his door. When he came to the door, [the errant Israelite] said to him, "What are you doing here, Phineas?" Phineas replied, "[I'm here to stop you!] Don't you see that the tribe of Levi—[my tribe]—is at all times responsible for the tribe of Simeon—[your tribe]?" [The man and woman] said to him, "Leave me alone! Perhaps the separatists have permitted this matter [after all]!"

When [Phineas] got in, the Holy, Blessed One performed six miracles:

The first miracle: Usually, [after intercourse] people separate from one another, but the angel of the Lord kept these two stuck together [so a single spear thrust could get them both].

The second miracle: [God] guided the spear directly into her belly, so that the man's penis would stick out. This made certain that nitpickers could not claim, "He, too, shouldered his way in and took care of himself."

The third miracle: The angel sealed their lips, so that they could not scream.

The fourth miracle: They did not slip off the point, but remained in place [when Phineas lifted them up on the spear.]

The fifth miracle: The angel raised the lintel so that [Phineas could carry] both of them out over his shoulder.

The sixth miracle: When he went out and saw the plague afflicting the people, what did he do? He threw them down to the ground and began to pray, as Scripture states, *"Phineas stepped forth and intervened, and the plague ceased"* (Ps. 106:30).

When the Israelites came to take vengeance against Midian, [for ensnaring them in sexual immorality], they found Balaam ben Beor. Why was he there? He had come to collect his salary for the 24,000 Israelites who had died in Shittim on his account.

Phineas said to him, "[Your salary?!] You didn't obey [God's] command to you nor did you do Balak's bidding: You didn't obey [God's] command to you—[God] said to you, 'You shall not go with the messengers of Balak,' but you went along with them. Nor did you do Balak's bidding—he said to you, 'Go curse Israel,' but you blessed them. But, for my part, I shall not withhold what's coming to you!"

This is in line with that which is written in Scripture: *"Together with the others that they slew, the Israelites put Balaam son of Beor, the augur, to the sword"* (Josh. 13:22).

What is the meaning of *"Together with the others that they slew"*? He was equal [in evil] to all the other slain put together.

Another interpretation: *"Together with the others that they slew"*—Just as their slain no longer have substance, so he had no substance, [for Phineas *did* withhold the cash owed him by the Midianites].

Another interpretation: *"Together with the others that they slew"*—Balaam hovered [in the air] over the slain, but when Phineas showed him the [priestly] frontlet, he fell down [to earth].

Another interpretation: *"Together with the others that they slew"*—this teaches that the Israelites paid him back in full and withheld nothing [of his punishment].

Doeg possessed great knowledge of Torah, [as the following illustrates]: The Israelites once asked [young] David, "What is the law as to the shewbread overriding the restrictions of the Sabbath?" He replied, "Arranging it overrides the restrictions of the Sabbath, [and so is permitted]; but kneading the dough and cutting it out do not override the restrictions of the Sabbath, [and must be done in advance]."

Doeg was there, and said, "Who dares to teach in my presence?" They told him, "It is David, son of Jesse." [As retribution for David's "insult,"] he immediately gave advice to Saul, King of Israel, to kill everyone in Nob, the city of the priests. As Scripture states: *"And the king commanded the guards standing by, 'Turn about and kill the priests of the LORD, for they are in league with David'. . . . [But the king's servants would not raise a hand to strike down the priests of the LORD]"* (1 Sam. 22:17). . . .

"Thereupon the king said to Doeg, 'You, Doeg, go and strike down the priests.' And Doeg the Edomite went and struck down the priests himself; that day he killed eighty-five men who wore the linen ephod" (1 Sam. 22:18). Now did not R. Ḥiyya teach, "They do not appoint two high priests at the same time"? [How could there be so many?] [Scripture here] teaches that all of them were worthy of [wearing the linen ephod, worthy of] the high priesthood.

How was [Doeg] ultimately dispatched?

R. Ḥaninah and R. Joshua b. Levi disputed: One of them said, "Fire burst forth from the house of the Holy of Holies and licked round about him." But the other one said, "His old students got together with him, and they were studying, but he forgot [his learning]. [This fulfills the verse,] '*The riches he swallows he vomits; God empties it out of his stomach*' (Job 20:15). [Given so clear a sign of his excommunication, the students killed him.]"

Ahithophel possessed powerful knowledge of Torah, [as the following three stories illustrate]:

It is written, "*David again assembled all the picked men of Israel, thirty thousand strong. [Then David and all the troops that were with him set out from Baalim of Judah to bring up from there the Ark of God to which the Name was attached, the name* LORD *of Hosts Enthroned on the Cherubim]*" (2 Sam. 6:1–2).

R. Berekhiah in the name of R. Abba bar Kahana: "David appointed ninety thousand elders on that day, but he did not appoint Ahithophel among them. As Scripture states: "*David again assembled all the picked men of Israel, thirty thousand strong*"—"*[David] assembled*" means "thirty;" and "*again*" means "thirty;" and Scripture explicitly speaks of thirty; that totals ninety thousand in all."

When David began to move the Ark of the Covenant of the LORD, he did not bear it in accord with the Torah: "*They loaded the Ark of God onto a new cart [and conveyed it from the house of Abinadab, which was on the hill; and Abinadab's sons, Uzza and Ahio, guided the new cart]*" (2 Sam. 6:3)—[since the Torah requires that priests carry the Ark, but not a cart,] the Ark kept raising the priests on high and dropping them, raising them up and dropping them.

David summoned Ahithophel and said to him, "Why don't you tell me what's going on—why does the Ark keep raising the priests up and cast them down to the ground?" [Ahitophel] replied, "Go ask the [ninety thousand] wise men you appointed!" Said David, "One who knows how to put an end to this, but does not do so, eventually will be put to death through strangulation." [Ahitophel] said to him, "Make a sacrifice before [the Ark], and it will stop." As Scripture states: "*When the bearers of the Ark of the* LORD *had moved forward six paces, he sacrificed an ox and a fatling*" (2 Sam. 6:13). . . .

Said the Holy, Blessed One to Ahithophel, "You purposely did not tell him the verse that any schoolchild knows: '*But to the Kohathites*

[Moses] did not give any [carts or oxen]; since theirs was the service of the most sacred objects, their porterage was by shoulder' (Num. 7:9)—yet you told him [to sacrifice]?!"

Similarly, when David set out to dig the foundations of the Temple, he dug fifteen hundred cubits and did not reach the earth's interior. Finally, he found a clay pot, and wanted to remove it. [The pot] said to him, "Don't do it!" [David] replied, "Why not?" [The pot] said, "For I am here to cover the great deep." [David] said to it, "How long have you been here?" [The pot] replied, "From the time that I heard the All Merciful at Sinai: *'I the LORD am your God'* (Exod. 20:2). [Since upon hearing God's voice] the earth shook and trembled, I am set here to seal the great deep."

Despite this, [David] did not obey; he removed the clay pot, and [the waters of] the great deep surged upward to flood the world. Ahithophel was standing there and said, "Just like that David will be suffocated and I shall become king!" Said David, "One who is a sage, who knows how to put an end to this, but does not do so, eventually will be put to death through strangulation." So [Ahithophel] said what he said and stopped up [the flood]. . . .

Despite [Ahithophel's obedient action], in the end he was strangled to death. Said R. Yose, "As the proverb says: 'A person ought to worry about the curse of a great person, even if it comes to naught.'"

R. Jeremiah in the name of R. Samuel bar Isaac, "Ahithophel once recited a scroll that Samuel passed to David, by means of the Holy Spirit."

What [other sorts of prophetic wonders] did Ahithophel do? When someone came to ask his advice, he would say, "Go do thus and such; if you don't trust me, then confirm things with the Urim and Thummim." Sure enough, if the man would go ask, he would find out that indeed matters were as [Ahitophel counseled]. As Scripture states: *"In those days, the advice which Ahitophel gave was accepted like an oracle sought [from God; that is how all the advice of Ahitophel was esteemed both by David and by Absalom]"* (2 Sam. 16:23). . . .

How was [Ahitophel] ultimately dispatched? *"When Ahitophel saw that his advice had not been followed, he saddled his ass [and went home to his native town. He set his affairs in order, and then he hanged himself. He was buried in his ancestral tomb]"* (2 Sam. 17:23).

Three deathbed testimonies did Ahithophel give his children: (1) "Do not rebel against the royal house of David, for you will find that the Holy, Blessed One favors them, especially in public [confrontations];" (2) "Do not have business dealings with someone on whom the hour smiles;" and (3) "If the day of Pentecost is bright, sow the best quality of wheat"—but they did not know whether he meant "bright" with dew or "bright" with sun.[12]

Let me provide an overview, so as to place matters in perspective. In Yerushalmi Sanhedrin 11:6, the rabbis equated three separate transgressions (idolatrous prophecy, fornication, and defamation of character) under the single rubric of "bearing false witness." All three transgressions involved the denial of the Torah's most basic commandments, and so were deemed punishable by death. In the complementary passage just presented, the rabbinic authors addressed the opposite end of the spectrum, namely, three men whose depth of Torah knowledge was truly miraculous. Whether addressing depravity or holiness, however, the Talmud makes its straightforward point: there is power in knowledge. By juxtaposing these passages, we point up the power of Torah.

Even the varied details of these stories—at least occasioned by discussion of the Ten Commandments—emphasize basic rabbinic viewpoints.

First, consider an assertion common to both Talmudic essays: Torah learning confers great powers upon those who possess it. Sages—rabbis—can work wonders. Phineas, for example, performed miracles because of his devotion to the Torah and to God alone. He defeated the idol-prophet and killed the Israelite who took an idolatress as wife. His knowledge of Scripture allowed Phineas to trap Balaam and so withhold his livelihood. And Phineas's actions against the blasphemous man and wife

---

12. For parallel passages, see B. Menahot 95a–b, B. Sukkah 53a–b, and B. Bava Batra 147a–b.

show the divine hand guided his spear. Torah knowledge leads to cunning and bravery, to miracle and valor.

A second point concerns the supernatural capabilities stemming from the Torah. These miraculous abilities operate even in the hands of an idolator, like Balaam, or an evil person, like Ahitophel. Only the special capacity conferred by Torah knowledge explains why an idol-prophet like Balaam was capable of levitating himself so as to view the slaughtered Israelites. Torah alone accounts for Ahitophel's exclusive knowledge both of the magical character of the Ark containing the Ten Commandments, and of the priestly oracles delivered by the Urim and Thummim. Furthermore, only the immediacy of Torah power explains why Ahitophel was able to rescue King David from certain death by drowning.

The surprising fact then is that "the devil may quote Scripture," and, if his knowledge is adequate, he benefits from the power of Torah. The knowledge gained from Torah thus seems to be amoral, certainly a shocking assertion.

And yet, these stories manage to rescue morality and its place in a Torah-centered theology. The true representatives of God's revelation can and will outdo those who wield the Torah's power immorally. So it is, for example, that Phineas easily brought Balaam down to earth from his magical levitation, merely by showing the priestly headpiece, the symbol of his appointment to serve God. Similarly, the Holy of Holies itself— earthly seat of God's revelation and judgment—punished Doeg the Edomite, for his murderous abuse of the mighty Torah power he had acquired. And, of course, a divine appointee, King David, so consistently dominated an evil sage that Ahitophel's last testament was: "Do not rebel against the royal house of David, for you will find that the Holy, Blessed One favors them, especially in public confrontations."

In sum, Torah grants powers to any who possess its secrets. But in the long run, only those who act with God's favor, in behalf of God's Commandments, are truly empowered and appointed to divine office.

The Ten Commandments and the History of Torah

Scripture provides an extended account of God's theophany and revelation at Sinai, including Moses' writing the Ten Commandments, breaking them, chiseling a second set of tablets, and presenting the Commandments to the Israelites, as well as a host of other details. In the rabbinic treatment of these stories about Moses' encounter with God, we find further clear statements of the meaning the rabbis find in the revelatory events. Of paramount importance is the way in which the Talmudic authors treat these events as removed from history. The "event" is transcended, rather than limited to the particular moment in time. In at least three cases, God's Ten Utterances appear in rabbinic lists of events taken entirely out of the timeline of history, and instead embedded in the calendar and its cycles.[13]

One such cycle involves the Sabbath as the pinnacle of weekly activity. In rabbinic theology, the Sabbath represents repose and rejoicing at the end of God's toil, and, of course, at the end of weekly labor by humanity, created in God's image and likeness.

Modern liturgical practice prescribes six Sabbath services, which form a theological cycle of their own. First, the rite of Welcoming the Sabbath (*Qabbalat Shabbat*) proclaims God as Sovereign and adjures his creations—both nature and humanity—to God's adoration.[14] Second, the Evening Service (*Maariv*) highlights God as Creator and urges God to sanctify Israel as the Sabbath itself is sanctified. Third, the Morning Service (*Shaharit*) continues the link to creation already established, but emphasizes the Sabbath as a sign of God's exclusive covenant with Israel, established both at creation and in the revelation at Sinai, represented in the public proclamation from the Torah scroll. Fourth, the Additional Service (*Musaf*), which explicitly replaces

---

13. See Jacob Neusner, *Messiah in Context: The Foundations of Judaism: Method, Theology, Doctrine* (Philadelphia, Pa.: Fortress, 1984), pp. 98–130, on the rabbinic use and conception of history.

14. See Abraham Joshua Heschel, *The Sabbath: Its Meaning for Modern Man* (New York: Farrar, Strauss, and Young, 1951), pp. 10, 95–101.

the Temple sacrifices originally offered on the Sabbath, accords central prominence to the Sinaitic revelation regarding proper Temple service and adjures God to redeem the Israelites so they may reinstitute the Sabbath offerings. Fifth, the Afternoon Service (*Minḥah*), in its Sabbath introduction, highlights God's absolute monotheism and the long-standing Sabbath observance of the Israelites, from Abraham on. Sixth and finally, the Rite of Separation (*Havdalah*) marks the formal end of Sabbath with prayers and intercessions for messianic redemption.

The Sabbath liturgical cycle just described has been fully in place since at least the late sixteenth century,[15] but the underlying theological structure certainly was known by early rabbinic times.[16] The cycle moves from Evening to Morning to Afternoon, emphasizing the flow of Creation (*Maariv*) into Revelation (*Shaharit* and *Musaf*), into Redemption (*Minḥah* and *Havdala*), and returning to Creation in the coming week. This cycle is a hallmark of the rabbinic Sabbath.[17]

Given the central role accorded to revelation in this Sabbath cycle, it should come as no surprise that the Ten Utterances—the paradigm of revelation—are somehow linked to the Sabbath. This turns out to be the case, although with a twist. As far as the rabbis were concerned, the Ten Utterances were an integral part of Sabbath, but in particular, of the seven days of creation commemorated in the Fourth Commandment, "Remember the Sabbath day and keep it holy." The passage of the

---

15. See Lawrence Hoffman, *The Canonization of the Synagogue Liturgy* (Notre Dame, Ind.: University of Notre Dame Press, 1979), pp. 72–89.

16. See, e.g., M. Taan. 4:3, which mentions three main Sabbath services, Morning, Additional, and Afternoon, as well as Hoffman, *Canonization of the Synagogue Liturgy*, pp. 72–73, for some of the differences between the Sabbath and daily prayer, which highlight the focus on creation (through the addition of Exod. 31:16–17), and redemption, through a protracted focus on God's kingdom and the punishment of sinners in the world to come.

17. On the themes of creation, revelation, and redemption, see Franz Rosenzweig, *The Star of Redemption*, English translation of the 2d ed. of 1930 by William W. Hallo (Notre Dame, Ind.: University of Notre Dame Press, 1985), pp. 93–261, esp. 112–13, 156–57, and 205.

Mishnah that follows asserts that the tablets were created just prior to that first Sabbath. The Ten Utterances, in other words, existed long before Sinai and revelation; they were, rather, part of God's original creation. In effect, this places the Ten Commandments in a new context: the miracle at Sinai was not one of revelation, but of creation!

Mishnah Avot 5:6

Ten things were created on the eve of the Sabbath at twilight, namely: (1) the mouth of the earth (Num. 16:32); (2) the mouth of the well (Num. 21:16–18); (3) the mouth of the ass (Num. 22:28); (4) the rainbow (Gen. 9:13); (5) the manna (Exod. 16:15); (6) the rod (Exod. 4:17); (7) the Shamir worm (M. Soṭ. 9:12); (8) letters; (9) writing; and (10) the tablets [of stone bearing the Ten Commandments] (Exod. 32:15).

In the brief paragraph from tractate Avot, the revelation of the Ten Commandments was set as the logical culmination of all creation, the tenth in a list of items brought into being just at twilight. The rabbis thus shifted away from the biblical account of revelation to a non-narrative setting. The tablets of stone were not solely the result of God's theophany (as Scripture implies; cf. Exod. 24:12, 31:18, and 32:16). The stone tablets were also a part of creation at the first. In the process of this shift, the rabbis managed to link the first two great themes of Judaic theology, creation and revelation.

The next, much longer Talmudic pericope joins these themes to the third focus, Israel's redemption. Once again, the Ten Utterances are subsumed in a list—not chronologially, but cyclically, ordered. This list corresponds to the yearly calendar, and specifically to the summer period of mourning for the many destructions inflicted on Israel.

The rabbis here eschew the more agricultural cycle found in the Bible. The Hebrew Bible organizes the yearly calendar around three pilgrimage festivals, each with an explicit connection to the planting and harvest cycle, as well as an implicit link to the historical emergence of Israel as a nation. First, Passover marks both the emergence of new buds in the spring and of Israel as a nation leaving Egypt (creation); the festival of Pentecost (*Shavuot*) represents the flowering of new grain in early summer, as well as the reception of Torah at Sinai, the flowering of Israel's spiritual life (revelation); and the festival of Tabernacles (*Sukkot*) highlights both the fullness of the fall harvest and Israel's acceptance of the yoke of the law, with its attendant possibility for salvation (redemption).

That cyclical scheme might reasonably have been invoked when speaking of the history of the Ten Commandments. Israel's desert wanderings and the divine production of *manna* could easily have been assimilated to the earth's bountiful spring crops, which emerge from winter destruction as if from a barren desert. And the Ten Commandments might well have been a crucial part of the early summer celebration of Sinaitic revelation at Shavuot. Nonetheless, the rabbis here utilize a different calendar, one not biblical but solely rabbinic. In this calendrical scheme, the crucial moments in the year are only two: three late summer weeks of mourning for the destroyed Temple, set against the winter celebration of Ḥanukkah, an eight-day rededication of the Temple.

The passage addresses itself to the summer mourning period, which lasts from the seventeenth of the Hebrew month Tammuz (July) to the ninth of Av (August). Here the Talmud fills out the story of when, how, and why Moses shattered the Tablets. Of at least passing importance is the role assigned to the sounds of idolatry. While Israel's idolatrous worship of the golden calf forms part of the biblical narrative, here the warning sounds find their importance in the larger rabbinic interest in anti-idolatrous narratives and legislation.

Mishnah Taanit 4:6 (4:5)

Five things befell our ancestors on the seventeenth of Tammuz and five on the ninth of Av:

On the seventeenth of Tammuz (1) the Tablets [of the Ten Commandments] were broken, (2) the Daily [Whole Offerings] ceased, (3) the city [of Jerusalem] was breached, (4) Apostomus burned [scrolls of] the Torah, and (5) an idol was set up in the sanctuary.

On the ninth of Av (1) it was decreed against our ancestors that they should not enter the Land of Israel, (2) the Temple was destroyed the first (3) and second time, (4) Betar was captured, and (5) the city [of Jerusalem] was ploughed up.

Yerushalmi Taanit 4:5 [Venice: 65b–c; Vilna: 22b–23b]

It is written, *"The Presence of the* Lord *abode on Mount Sinai, and the cloud hid it for six days. On the seventh day [God] called to Moses from the midst of the cloud"* (Exod. 24:16). [Immediately prior, Scripture says]: *"When Moses had ascended . . . "* (Exod. 24:15). The [voice of the Lord came to Moses] on the seventh day, [the day] after the declaration of the Ten Utterances, and at the beginning of the forty [days that Moses would spend on the Mountain]. [That is, the Utterances were given on the sixth of Sivan, and the next day—the seventh of Sivan—began Moses' forty days on Sinai.]

Moses said to the people, "I am going to spend forty days on the mountain." When the fortieth day, [erroneously counting from the sixth, not the seventh of Sivan], had passed, and Moses did not return: *"When the people saw that Moses was so long in coming down from the mountain . . . "* (Exod. 32:1a). When the sixth hour had passed, and he did not return: *" . . . the people gathered themselves against Aaron and said to him, 'Come, make us a god who shall go before us, [for that man Moses, who brought us from the land of Egypt—we do not know what has happened to him]'"* (Exod. 32:1b). [So] *"The* Lord *spoke to Moses, 'Hurry down, for your people, [whom you brought out of the land of Eqypt,] have acted basely'"* (Exod. 32:7).

"When Joshua heard the sound of the people in its boisterousness, he said to Moses, 'There is a cry of war in the camp'" (Exod. 32:17). Moses thought, "Here is a man who is destined to act as governor of 600,000 people, yet he does not know the difference between one sound and another!" *"[So Moses] answered, 'It is not the sound of the tune of triumph, or the sound of the tune of defeat; It is the sound of song that I hear!'"* (Exod. 32:18). Said R. Yose, "[Moses implied], 'It is the sound of the praise of idols that I hear.'" . . .

. . . *"As soon as Moses came near the camp and saw the calf and the dancing, [he became enraged; and he hurled the tablets from his hands and shattered them at the foot of the mountain]"* (Exod. 32:19). R. Ḥilqiah in the name of R. Aḥa: "On the basis of [Moses' example], we learn that one should not reach judgment on the basis of guesswork, [but only after seeing the facts first hand]." . . .

. . . *"[As soon as Moses came near the camp and saw the calf and the dancing], he became enraged; and he hurled the Tablets from his hands and shattered them at the foot of the mountain"* (Exod. 32:19). R. Ishmael taught, "The Holy, Blessed One told him to break them: *'I will inscribe on the Tablets the Commandments that were on the first Tablets that you smashed, and you shall deposit them in the Ark'* (Deut. 10:2)—it is as if [God] said to him, 'You did the right thing in breaking them.'"

R. Samuel bar Naḥman in the name of R. Jonathan: "The Tablets were six handbreadths long and three broad. Moses held on to two handbreadths, and the Holy, Blessed One held on to two, with a space of two handbreadths in the middle. When the Israelites did that [terrible] deed, the Holy, Blessed One wanted to grab them from Moses [and take back the gift of Torah]. But Moses was stronger and he seized them from [God]. Thus Scripture praises Moses at the end [of the Pentateuch]: *'[Never again did there arise in Israel a prophet like Moses— whom the LORD singled out, face to face], . . . for all the great might and awesome power [that Moses displayed before all Israel]'* (Deut. 34:12). [So God says], 'May the one who was stronger than I prosper.'"

R. Yoḥanan in the name of R. Yose bar Abayye said to him, "The tablets wanted to flee [at the sight of the golden calf], but Moses was holding on to them: *'Thereupon I gripped the two Tablets . . .'"* (Deut. 9:17).

It was taught in the name of R. Neḥemiah, "The writing itself flew off [the Tablets]." R. Ezra in the name of R. Judah b. R. Simon, "The Tablets were a burden weighing forty *seahs,* and the writing was holding them up. When the writing flew off, the Tablets became too heavy for Moses, and fell and were broken. . . . "

. . . . R. Simeon b. Yoḥai taught, "R. Aqiva, my master, interpreted as follows: *'Thus said the LORD of Hosts: The fast of the fourth month, the fast of the fifth month, the fast of the seventh month, and the fast of the tenth month shall become occasions for joy and gladness, happy festivals for the House of Judah; but you must love honesty and integrity'* (Zech. 8:19).

"'The fast of the fourth month' refers to: *On the seventeenth of Tammuz (1) the Tablets [of the Ten Commandments] were broken, (2) the Daily [Whole*

Offerings] ceased, (3) the city [of Jerusalem] was breached, (4) Apostomus burned [scrolls of] the Torah, and (5) an idol was set up in the sanctuary (M. Taan. 4:6).[18]

The passage breaks roughly into three sections. Discussion opens with attention to historical facts: the Talmud fixes the sixth of Sivan as the day on which the Ten Commandments initially were revealed, the seventh of Sivan as the first of Moses' forty days on Mount Sinai, and the seventeenth of Tammuz as the day he returned, saw Israel's idol, and shattered the stones bearing God's words. But the rabbis' historical attention here was not calendrical, looking toward the setting through time, but cyclical, paying attention to the the season of year. The rabbis focused on the Sinai event as an ongoing, yearly commemoration, not as a mere one-time occurrence.

A second segment describes the Tablets of the law in terms of size and weight, and narrates the tug-of-war between God and Moses when Moses wanted to break the Tablets. Aimed sharply at the aspect of revelation itself, here the rabbis added depth and specificity first to the granting, and second to the taking away, of the pristine divine command.

Finally, the Talmud speaks of the seventeenth of Tammuz, the day of mourning for the loss of the Tablets (as well as for the breaching of Jerusalem's city wall and other destructions). It would be difficult to have predicted the rabbinic attitude, which took Zechariah's prophecy of restoration as the critical exegetical tool for understanding the theological cycle. It is, however, precisely this ironic twist that reveals the broad sweep of the rabbinic approach. By commanding that this day of fasting be one of rejoicing at the impending redemption of all Israel, the rabbis showed that the historical events all pointed in a single direction. The ultimate redemption of the Israelites would be accomplished through their return to Sinai and even to the origins of revelation that derived from creation itself.

---

18. For parallel passages, see B. Taanit 26a, 28b, B. Sanhedrin 102a, and B. Shabbat 87a.

In speaking of the history of Torah, then, the rabbinic authors found in God's giving of Torah the means for the return to Sinaitic revelation. The Ten Utterances corresponded, in their multiple meanings, to three paramount theological values: *Creation* was represented by the Ten Commandments themselves, made just at twilight before God rested on the first Sabbath. *Revelation* found its place in the rabbis' calendrical accounts of Moses' and Israel's meeting with God at Sinai. The seventeenth of Tammuz was made to symbolize destruction—of creation, of the law itself—due to Israel's inability to uphold the First and Second Commandments. But through rabbinic exegesis, destruction was overturned into the incipient *Redemption* and salvation of Israel and Zion. The Ten Utterances, therefore, revealed a fully articulated theological scheme, in which God's acts in relation to humanity and the people of Israel—acts of creation, revelation, and redemption—smoothly integrated one with another.

Further evidence of their treatment of the Ten Utterances within this transhistorical scheme is to be found in the rabbis' utilization of the events surrounding the Decalogue's revelation as an explanatory device. At issue in the following passage, which concludes this chapter, is the biblical rite of piercing a slave's ear (Exod. 21:2–6). This act binds the slave to a master beyond the six years normally allowed by statute.

Mishnah Qiddushin 1:2

A Hebrew slave may be acquired through money or a writ; he acquires his [freedom] through [the passage of] years, at the Jubilee [year], or by deduction from the purchase price [redeeming himself at his outstanding value (Lev. 25:50–51)].

The Hebrew slave girl has an advantage over him, for she acquires her [freedom in the above stated manners, as well as] through the appearance of tokens [of puberty].

The slave whose ear is pierced is acquired through an act of piercing the ear (Exod. 21:5); he acquires his [freedom] only at the Jubilee [year] or at the death of his master.

Yerushalmi Qiddushin 1:2 [Venice: 59d; Vilna: 11b]

It was taught: R. Eliezer b. Jacob says, "Why is a slave brought to the door [to have his ear pierced, when about to enter into lifetime servitude]? [The door is the appropriate place to bind the slave in perpetuity] because through [blood placed over the lintel of the Israelites'] doors [in Egypt] they went forth from slavery to freedom."

His disciples asked Rabban Yohanan b. Zakkai, "Why is it that this slave has his ear pierced, rather than any other of his limbs?" He gave them [two answers], "At Mount Sinai, his ear heard, '*You shall have no other gods besides Me*' (Exod. 20:3); yet [the slave] threw off the yoke of heavenly dominion and accepted instead a dominion made by flesh and blood, [namely, the golden calf]. [Similarly], at Mount Sinai, his ear heard, '*For it is to Me that the Israelites are servants; [they are my servants, whom I freed from the land of Egypt, I the* LORD *your God]*' (Lev. 25:55); yet [the slave] took another master for himself. Therefore, let his ear be pierced [as a sign of perpetual servitude], for it did not obey what it heard."

The rabbis' principal contribution here was the thorough absorption of the slave rite into the larger theological system. Within the rabbinic worldview, even the seemingly trivial act of retaining a slave for lifetime service took its meaning from the Sinaitic theophany. Just as the Ten Commandments were first given and then the Tablets withdrawn due to the nation's idolatry and proclaiming a god of mere gold, so, too, slavery became possible because the nation ignored the First Commandment, taking in God's place human masters.

The history of Torah—in the case of the Ten Utterances, mapped to creation, revelation, and redemption—thus represented more than a few distinct events. For the rabbis, these constituted paradigms for the actions and beliefs of future generations, not mere moments in the past. In establishing these theological links between the generations, Torah takes on an ever more vital role in everyday life as it ties mundane existence to the revelation at Sinai. Its claim of authority stems from the transhistorical perspective of rabbinism, which allows those who reside in the here and now to participate in and return to the Sinaitic revelation. Therein lies Judaism's claim upon modern Jews: to the extent that they emulate and understand the rabbis and their theology, they transcend their particular moment in history. The Ten Utterances command not just the ancient Israelites at Sinai, but all who stand with them in the weekly and yearly celebration of that revelation.

5. In Search of Rabbinic Authority for Scripture

The Ten Utterances in the Talmudic materials we have examined thus far exemplify the early rabbinic use of the Oral and Written Law in the development of their theological inquiry. In detailing the perils of idolatry, the Ten Utterances provided an opportunity to discuss the power and history of Torah. Such wide-ranging explorations raise an important consideration. The rabbis used scriptural materials in a variety of ways, and in so doing, they turned to a variety of sources for the authority that undergirded their law. Biblical materials alone could not have sufficed, for a myriad of unforeseen cases might arise to thwart reading the Bible simply as an eternal rule book.

We have already seen how problems might ensue if, for example, a single Commandment were to be considered independently of the larger rabbinic hermeneutical framework. When one of the rabbis ruled that a person must not directly attempt to recover stolen property, so as to avoid the appearance of being a thief (see Yerushalmi Sanhedrin 8:3, presented in chapter 3 of this volume), he refused to allow practical matters to take their course. Such an adherence merely to the principle (theft is prohibited), but not to the larger purpose of the law (respect and preservation of private property), could quickly lead to an untenable moral and legal morass.[1] People simply would not be able to recover what was rightfully theirs, because a scriptural rule prohibited this.

---

1. This type of problem is neatly summarized, together with a plea for integrated and case-sensitive moral reasoning, in Albert R. Jonsen and Stephen Toulmin, *The Abuse of Casuistry* (Berkeley: University of California Press, 1988), pp. 5–11.

In contrast to this stringent application of unwavering principle (issued, after all, by a single sage in opposition to the full rabbinic consistory), rabbinic legal and ethical reasoning usually did not confine itself to a single mode of argument. Instead, the rabbis promoted an integrated system of law and morality, in which any legitimate source of authority could illuminate a given question. In the broadest context of Jewish law, the rabbis' strategy was to demonstrate the interdependence of the Oral and Written Torahs, without devaluing the norms or authority of either. The Ten Utterances, for instance, must be allowed to stand as absolute law, the clear-cut statement of Jewish ethics and belief; yet the rabbis required a means to decide the relevant law in cases where a narrow application of the Ten Commandments might result in disastrous effects.

This chapter will demonstrate that the rabbis employed a consistent principle of decision. When confronted with clear-cut cases of law, the rabbis turned directly to Scripture. The revealed law, in this sense, was foundational, limning the acts appropriate in any number of elementary circumstances. For example, premeditated infanticide is prohibited by the Decalogue's admonition against murder, since the rabbis recognized that an infant is a person entitled to the protection of this law (see, for example, Mishnah Ohalot 7:6). But what would be the rabbis' approach to cases in which the biblical law does not so directly address the precise situation at hand? Here the rabbis derived their discussion from principles that underlay the Bible's rulings and the oral tradition. That is to say, the Written Torah serves to provide guidance, but in complicated conundrums cannot by itself suffice. For instance, the question of abortion forms the counterpart to the issue of infanticide, just mentioned. The Decalogue's prohibition against murder cannot so easily apply to abortion, for, by rabbinic standards, a fetus is not yet fully a person and hence cannot be the victim of a murder. How, then, did the rabbis decide whether to permit an abortion? Principles by which to decide the legality of abortion must be teased out of biblical materials concerning the conflicting rights of persons of unequal social status. Since no simple biblical rule here applies, the rabbis would proceed on a case-by-case basis, weighing the mother's and the fetus' claims, and then arriving at a decision.[2] The contrasting cases of infanticide and abortion show that, if Scripture and its particular admonitions are accorded primacy in rabbinic ethics, the final goal is, nonetheless, to promote the underlying principles revealed at Sinai.

Types of Ethical Argument

Justifications for a particular rule and the authority that stands behind it form one principal interest of the Talmud of the Land of Israel. David Weiss Halivni speaks of this tendency toward justified law, which characterizes much of rabbinic literature, as follows:

What all these have in common—[biblical] motive clauses, *Midreshei Halakhah* [early works of scriptural exegesis], and *Gemara* [i.e., the two Talmuds]—is their proclivity for vindicatory law, for law that is justified, against law that is autocratically prescribed. This proclivity is, to be sure, not shared equally. Most laws in the Bible do not have supporting motive clauses. The hermeneutic justification of the *Midreshei Halakhah* is not as vindicatory as the usual logical reasoning of the *Gemara*. Yet in contrast with the apodictic Mishnah, they all seem to have a preference for law that is expressly reasonable, that seeks to win the hearts of those to whom it is addressed. They seem to convey that Jewish law cannot be imposed from above, to be blindly observed. Jewish law is justificatory, often revealing its own *raison d'être*.[3]

---

2. See David M. Feldman, *Marital Relations, Birth Control, and Abortion in Jewish Law: An Examination of the Rabbinic Legal Tradition that Underlies Jewish Values with Regard to Marriage, Sex, and Procreation, with Comparative Reference to Christian Tradition* (New York: Schocken Books, 1978; originally published 1968), pp. 262–67, 275–94.
3. David Weiss Halivni, *Midrash, Mishnah, and Gemara: The Jewish Predilection for Justified Law* (Cambridge, Mass.: Harvard University Press, 1986), p. 4.

Halivni's point, made implicitly in his claim that *halakhah* tries to win the hearts and minds of its students, is that a fully articulated Talmudic argument is a form of training. The spirit of rabbinic law lies, then, in this: legal discourse educates and elevates one to new levels of holiness or *qedushah*, both in act and in intellect.

Rabbinic materials regarding a given Commandment thus determine, finally, how Jews will integrate the rule into their daily lives. The medium is the message; or more precisely, it is part of the message, to be combined with the details of prescribed and proscribed activities. Only when students understand the justification for the biblical and rabbinic law do they grasp the larger rabbinic mind to which the Talmud testifies.

These deeper principles allow us to begin to appreciate the "basic norms"[4] behind the rabbis' understanding of biblical injunctions. An example ought to clarify the distinction between a simple injunction and the basic norm it expresses. The Bible prohibits fraud with the simple statement, "When you sell property to your neighbor . . . , you shall not wrong one another" (Lev. 25:14). But the rabbis strive to supply a fuller rationale, which Jacob Neusner has paraphrased in this manner: "The task of society is to maintain perfect stasis, to preserve the prevailing situation, and to secure the stability of all relationships."[5] This underlying norm, when expressed in concrete law, gives rise to details of rabbinic legislation against fraud, for in any transaction merchants are enjoined to state clearly the fair market value, and at least de jure, set prices within one-sixth of that value. But a stability norm explains more than antifraud legislation; it also stands behind most rabbinic law concerning civil society and the government's role in everyday activity. By seeking the validating, basic norm for a simple rabbinic rule—the prohibition against fraud—we have uncovered

---

4. David Little and Sumner B. Twiss, *Comparative Religious Ethics: A New Method* (San Francisco, Calif.: Harper & Row, 1978), pp. 103–9.
5. Neusner, *Judaism: The Evidence of the Mishnah*, p. 144.

an important element in rabbinic political philosophy—the stability principle vis à vis personal property, which is part of a larger order in which all things belong, ultimately, to God. In general, this search allows us to perceive the basic elements of rabbinic theology, which are contained in discrete rulings.

Yet discovery of the principles underlying rabbinic law provides a second benefit. On the basis of these principles, we may analyze the mode of moral argumentation used by the Talmud's authors.[6] What constitutes a valid moral concern, and how does a particular concern point toward the larger whole, the spirit of the law? What relative weights are assigned to various matters as the discourse on a given halakhic issue proceeds in guiding its readers?

In our investigation of the Ten Utterances in rabbinic law, we must attend to two matters, entirely coordinated with one another: the *content* of moral arguments—which adumbrates deeper principles of rabbinic theology—and the *mode* of moral argument—which flows from the content and reinforces it within the mind of nascent rabbinism. Particularly evident to the rabbis of the Talmud, as we shall see, was Scripture's direct force, which could authorize an entire body of law with a single word. So, too, the force of human experience energized rabbinic legislation, imploring action consonant with simple logic and the behaviors of everyday life. And, finally, the rabbis understood the overwhelming impact of moral precedent, found in the actions and mannerisms of great rabbinic leaders and scholars. In the intersection of these three—Scripture, experience, and moral example—we will find the uniquely rabbinic approach to holiness, or what in modernity might be termed ethics.

---

6. A classical formulation of modes of ethical argumentation is found in C.D. Broad, *Five Types of Ethical Theory* (London: Routledge and Kegan Paul, 1956; originally published 1930). For the most part, the rabbis utilize all means of argument; it is rather the overall structure and hierarchy of their discourse that is illuminating.

Of course, these three sources of authority were not equally utilized by the rabbinic authors. They are arranged rather in a pedagogical hierarchy that begins with one type of argument and only then guides its students to others. To anticipate what we shall find, the rabbis tended to bypass mere prooftexting as a superficial reliance upon Scripture's authority. It is as if someone might object, "Fine, the Bible tells me to revere the Sabbath. But what is the full impact of that command?" In answer to this question, the rabbis developed a sense of authority based largely upon the lives and deeds of rabbis held up as moral exemplars. People ought to behave in certain ways because the great men of the age act in just that manner. The rabbis also found precedent for ethical behavior in nature and the physical world. And, having pointed out such guideposts to proper behavior, the rabbis introduce Scripture not through mere prooftexting, but because according to rabbinic theology the Hebrew Bible is the one authentic repository of fact, logic, and understanding about the world. In determining Jewish law, then, God's revealed Word is one of the paramount clues to proper activity. The following passages, while confined to rabbinic discourse on the Ten Utterances and their legal validations, nevertheless exemplify Talmudic thought in general.

Rabbinic Authority and Moral Example

Within the entire Talmud of the Land of Israel, the clearest essay relevant to the authority behind a particular Utterance concerns honor of father and mother. As we have seen in several instances, the Mishnah speaks of the Commandment within one of its lists, here specifying actions to be performed without limit, and for which one earns rewards both in this world and in the world to come.

Mishnah Peah 1:1

These are things that are not [subject to a specific] measure: (1) The [quantity of produce set aside as] the corner offering (see Lev. 19:9),

(2) the [quantity of produce designated as] first fruits, [and brought to the Temple on Pentecost (see Deut. 26:1–11)], (3) the [value of the] appearance [offering, brought to Jerusalem on each of the three pilgrimage festivals (see Deut. 16:16–17)], (4) the [quantity of] righteous deeds [performed], and (5) [time spent in] study of Torah.

These are things the benefits of which a person enjoys in this world, while the principal remains for him in the world to come: (1) [deeds done in] honor of father and mother, (2) [performance of] righteous deeds and (3) acts that bring about peace between one person and another. But (4) study of Torah is equal to all of them together.

While the Fifth Utterance is mentioned only in the middle of the second list, it occasions a rather broad Talmudic discourse.[7] The opening portion of the essay, which addresses the use of moral paradigm, falls into three structural layers, slowly but ever more precisely delimiting the spirit of the law. The internal dynamic moves from discussion of non-Jews in relationship to their parents, to Jews in relation to theirs. The passage thus opens with stories of the gentile Chief Councillor of Ashkelon, named Dama ben Natina, and the great reverence he had for his parents. The Talmud here invokes purely consequentialist arguments that anyone might understand. The essay then moves inward, by contrasting two famous sages, Rabbi Tarfon and Rabbi Ishmael. In using stories about these great rabbis, the Talmud shows the limits of parental reverence and impudence, but also more directly addresses the individual Jew following rabbinic dictates. In these paradoxical arguments, the rabbis point up the absolute authority of the biblical commandment: even in ridiculous circumstances, one must follow one's parents' desires vis-à-vis their respect. Third and finally, the precedent is brought home to the student, in hypothetical ac-

---

7. In the early parts of this large unit of discourse, note that the Talmud's discussion seems to imply that honor of father and mother should have been included in the first list at M. Peah 1:1, which specifies actions not subject to specific limits. This, of course, is in addition to its inclusion in the second list, actions for which one earns double rewards.

counts revealing the rights and obligations that bind parent and child in close relationship. By so guiding the student along these lines, the Talmud advocates performance of the law willingly and with the proper intent. It shows not only the material benefits of submitting to the law, but also the eternal rewards derived from upholding the underlying principles of parental respect.

Notice that the Talmudic authors, in seeking to teach, eschewed a blanket principle to guide respectful behavior toward parents. Instead, they moved casuistically, allowing proper action in each case to instruct the reader. To allow for better understanding of each unit that follows, I present the three contiguous sections of the Talmud's essay separately.

Dama ben Natina as Paradigm

In the stories about Dama ben Natina and his parents that open the discourse, the validating argument for respect of parents is postponed until the conclusion. But the sheer riches Dama acquires in exchange for respecting his parents suggest that similar honorific behavior likewise will draw in its wake beneficial consequences and instant rewards.[8]

Yerushalmi Peah 1:1 [Venice: 15c–d; Vilna: 3a–4a]

. . . R. Abbahu in the name of R. Yoḥanan: "They asked R. Eliezer, 'How far must one go in honor of father and mother?'

"He said to them, 'You're asking me? Go ask Dama ben Natina, [someone known for the great lengths to which he went in honor of his father and mother].'"

[The Talmud now cites several stories about Dama ben Natina to show to what length one must go in honor of his father and mother:]
(1) Dama ben Natina was the chief of the city councillors. One time

---

8. For an extended analysis of Pentateuchal narratives in terms of positive-consequentialist reasoning, seeking always the best possible outcomes, see Steven J. Brams, *Biblical Games: A Strategic Analysis of Stories in the Old Testament* (Cambridge, Mass.: The MIT Press, 1980).

his mother hit him in front of all the councillors, and the slipper [with which she hit him] fell out of her hand. [Dama had so much respect for his mother that] he reached [and picked up the slipper] for her, so that she would not have to trouble herself [to pick it up].

(2) Said R. Hezekiah, "There was a gentile from Ashkelon [i.e., Dama ben Natina], who was chief of the city councillors. [He had so much respect for his father that] during his entire life, he never sat upon the stone seat upon which his father used to sit. [Furthermore], when his father died, he deemed the stone his god [in his father's honor]."

(3) One time, the Jaspis - [stone], corresponding to the tribe of Benjamin [in the high priest's breastplate], was lost. [The sages] said, "Does anyone have a gemstone like this? [If so, we can purchase it and replace the Jaspis.]" Others replied, "Dama ben Natina has one like that." They went to him and agreed to pay him one hundred *dinars*. He went out to bring them the stone, and came upon his father, who was sleeping. Some say the key to his jewelry box was attached to his father's finger. Others say his father's feet were resting upon the jewelry box. [In either case, lest he disturb his father's sleep, Dama would not take the stone out of the box.] [Dama] returned and said to them, "I cannot bring [the stone] to you." [Misinterpreting Dama's action, the sages] said, "Perhaps he wants more money, [so] let us raise [our offer] to two hundred or maybe to a thousand *dinars*." [Still Dama would not bring them the stone, for fear of waking his father.] When his father awoke from his slumber, [Dama] went and brought [the gem to the sages]. They wanted to give him the amount they last offered him, but he would not accept this [from them]. He said, "Now shall I sell you my father's honor for money? I will not make a profit at all from honoring my father!" [Dama therefore sold them the stone for the original price offered, one hundred *dinars*.]

How did the Holy, Blessed One pay [Dama] a reward [for honoring his father in this way]? Said R. Yose b. R. Bun, "That very night, his cow gave birth to a red heifer, [a very rare, valuable specimen suitable for use in the rite of purification described at Num. 19:2–13]. The entire Israelite [nation] paid him [the cow's] weight in gold, and bought [the red cow]."

Said R. Shabtai, "[This third story accords with that which] is written [in Scripture], '[*Shaddai—we cannot attain thereto; God] is great in power and justice. And [God] does not torment those abundant in righteous-*

ness' (Job 37:23)—[which means] the Holy, Blessed One does not delay paying the reward to a [righteous] gentile who performs a religious duty [incumbent only upon Israelites]."[9]

These tales systematically illustrate the dual point of the Mishnah's lists. Dama went to extreme lengths to honor his mother and father, and for this received ample monetary compensation directly from God. The Talmud's treatment of the Fifth Utterance is in line with the fundamental book of rabbinic theology, the Mishnah. The rabbinic discourses, in other words, expanded upon honor of parents in ways that have little or no apparent relation to the Bible itself.

At the outset, the rabbis did not invoke biblical themes such as inheritance of the land eternally (Exod. 20:12), or other discussions of filial piety carrying forward the Hebrew Bible's concerns. As has often been noted of rabbinic discourse, Scripture does supply a few relevant facts, crucial details of everyday life taken from the Bible and used within the rabbis' arguments:[10] the Jaspis stone, the high priest's breastplate, and the tribe of Benjamin all stem from Exodus 28:15–30 and Leviticus 8:6–9, while the red heifer is a straightforward reference to Numbers 19:1–21. Yet if Scripture here supplied facts, it is the rabbis who created the narratives invoked as authoritative. Only at the end of the tales, in discussing the reward paid to Dama, do we have clear deference to Scripture: such rewards, it is asserted, serve as an illustration that "God does not torment those abundant in righteousness," but rather rewards such gentiles forthwith. Still, Job 37:23 bears no relation whatsoever to the overarching

---

9. Tractate Peah has appeared in a new critical edition: Adin Steinsaltz, *The Talmud Yerushalmi: Tractate Peah. Explained, Translated, and Pointed,* Hebrew (Jerusalem: The Israel Institute for Talmudic Publications, 1987). My translations here are based upon that edition, pp. 23–30. See also Roger Brooks, *Talmud of the Land of Israel,* vol. 2, *Tractate Peah,* ad loc., for textual notes. Cf. Y. Qid. 1:7 where this entire unit reappears with slight variations and additions; for other parallel passages, see B. Qiddushin 31a–b and B. Avodah Zarah 23a–b.

10. See, e.g., Jacob Neusner, *Judaism in Society,* pp. 78–79.

theme of honoring parents and is cited here because of its relevance to rewards paid to gentiles, an important, but nonetheless tangential, concern.

If reliance upon God's direct commanding revelation does not serve to open the issue of parental honor, it is because of Rabbi Eliezer's surprising response. He diverted attention to a well-known gentile political figure, and alleged that this man's economic success stemmed from the scrupulous honors he paid his parents: ignoring his mother's spanking, never disturbing his father's sleep, even idolizing his favorite chair. In this opening segment of the Talmud's essay, the locus of authority is to be found not in God's words, contained in the Bible, but in the actions of, and rewards paid to, an ordinary person for his actions (in his case, above and beyond the call of duty) in fulfilling God's law.

The underlying argument for the reader of such stories is a simple quid pro quo: if one respects mother and father in an unlimited manner (as did Dama ben Natina), then God will pay out monetary and eternal compensation. The appeal for authority is based on a consequentialist calculation: what rewards may be expected by a respectful child? The argument aims directly at the pocketbook, if not also at the promise of an extended portion in the afterlife.

Rabbi Ṭarfon and Rabbi Ishmael as Paradigms

The next segment of this extended discussion asserts that parents alone—and often capriciously—may determine just what actions are deemed respectful. These two great sages see their task as fulfilling God's commands; but their mothers' desires and requests flesh out the spirit of the rule and complete the Commandment. The mothers here act in part *in loco Dei*, as the authority that defines proper action.

Yerushalmi Peah 1:1 (continued)

R. Ṭarfon's mother went down for a walk in her courtyard on the Sabbath. [Her slipper came off, and she would not retie it, because that would be a violation of Sabbath laws]. R. Tarfon, [not wanting his mother's feet to become sore], went and placed his two hands under her feet, so that she could walk upon them all the way to her couch.

Some time later, [R. Tarfon] became ill, and the sages came in to visit him. [His mother] said to them, "Pray for Tarfon my son, for he treats me with far too much respect!" They said to her, "What did he do for you?" She told them [the foregoing] story. They said to her, "Even if he were to do so thousands of thousands [of times], still he would not attain even half [the measure] that the Torah commands [for honor of one's mother]!"

R. Ishmael's mother came and complained against [her son] before our rabbis. She said to them, "Rebuke Ishmael my son, for he does not treat me with respect!" At that moment our rabbis' faces flushed [with embarrassment]. They thought, "Is it possible that R. Ishmael would not treat his parents with respect?" [So] they said to her, "What did he do to you?" She said, "When he left the [scholars'] meeting place I wanted to wash his feet and drink the water, but he wouldn't let me, [thereby showing me disrespect]!" They said to [Ishmael], "Since this is her wish, this is [what you must do as a mode of] honoring her."

[With regard to the foregoing stories], said R. Mana, "The millers have spoken well: 'Each person's merit is within his own basket.'" [I.e., each person produces an amount of flour dependent not upon the *amount* of grain he harvests, but the *quality* of grain he happens to process. In the present context, this means that the value of Tarfon's and Ishmael's deeds depends not upon the amount of respect with which they treated their mothers, but upon their mothers' perceptions of their actions.]

[Thus, when] R. Tarfon's mother told them [the aforementioned events, namely, that her son treated her with too much respect, the sages] replied to her thus, [that he had not treated her with enough respect]. [And when] R. Ishmael's mother told them [the aforementioned events, namely, that her son was disrespectful], they replied to him thus, [that he must treat her in accord with her wishes, however disgusting he might find them].

[Throughout much of his life], R. Zeira was troubled and said, "Would that I had a mother and father, whom I could honor and thereby inherit the Garden of Eden!" [But] when he heard these two stories, he said, "Praise God that I have neither father nor mother; I am not capable of acting like R. Ṭarfon, nor could I tolerate what R. Ishmael tolerated!"

Said R. Avun, "I am exempt from the religious duty of honoring father and mother."

[In explanation of Avun's statement], they said, "When his mother conceived him, his father died. When she gave birth to him, his mother died." [Since Avun's parents never were alive during his lifetime, he never had to meet the obligation of honoring them.][11]

These two stories, which move the discussion from the gentile, Dama ben Natina, to the examples set by Rabbi Ishmael and Rabbi Ṭarfon, complement one another on several levels. One presents a son who is too deferential, the other a son who refused to do his mother's bidding. One represents a son who acts for the sake of parental respect, the other a son who refrains from acting. And both sons, ultimately, are frustrated in their efforts to fulfill the Fifth Commandment. So the Talmud, once again in line with the Mishnah, emphasized the extreme lengths to which one must go in honor of parents.

But in contrast to the simple monetary rewards validating Dama's acts, here we find greater credence given to authoritarian justification. One source of such authority, as I noted, rests with the parents themselves. Since respect can be so subjective a matter, parents may determine what suffices as proper conduct for their children, even if such behaviors seem excessive or disrespectful. Yet throughout the stories, such parental discretion is compared to a separate standard, indicating a larger source of authority. References to "not even half of what the Torah commands" imply that the absolute nature of respecting parents rests in the Sinaitic revelation. It is the Torah that commands honor of parents, and individuals must, by definition, follow its dictates.

Yet a broader view of the meaning of Torah, as I advocated in chapter 4, likewise moves our attention from Scripture to

---

11. For a parallel passage, see B. Qiddushin 31b.

rabbinism, so that the authoritative, commanding voice is not God's alone, but that of the halakhic process in which the rabbis participated. After all, we know *how* to honor our parents not because Scripture specifies this or that detail, but because of rabbinic precedent. The deeds (or, more precisely, the misdeeds) of Rabbis Ishmael and Ṭarfon determine the scope of the Commandment and instruct students of their obligations.

If narrowly understood, "what the Torah commands" refers to the Pentateuch (and to the Ten Commandments) and highlights the divine command; still the phrase has an unmistakable resonance. In rabbinic literature, the authority of Torah is coextensive with the entire legal enterprise. The rabbis, after all, applied the law so as to determine what Scripture means in terms of concrete actions for Judaic life.

It follows that the major source of authority here is a confident rabbinic legal system, not mere fundamentalistic Bible study. And Rabbi Zeira, at the end of the two contrasting tales, supplied the rabbinic justification for respecting one's parents: "Would that I had a mother and father, whom I could honor and thereby inherit the Garden of Eden!" Despite his personal foibles, Rabbi Zeira pointed out the paradisiacal consequences of upholding the law. In the first two units of this larger essay, then, the rabbis connect Scripture's commanding voice with a typical, practical rabbinic concern for the consequences of one's acts, both in the here and now and in the hereafter.

"Disrespect" as Paradigm

A final set of paradigmatic stories utilizes paradoxical arguments to emphasize the true nature of respect for parents. Having already shown that the consequences of one's actions are an important validating concern (à la Dama ben Natina) and, furthermore, that one must submit fully to the divine command, even in farfetched cases (like Rabbis Ṭarfon and Ishmael), the editors of the Talmud now move to close their paradigmatic arguments. The rabbinic preference for the intentions accompanying one's actions predominate here.

Yerushalmi Peah 1:1 (continued)

There is [one type of fellow] who feeds his father fattened [animals, of high quality, suitable for use in the Temple rites], yet [despite honoring his father in this way], receives Gehenna as his inheritance. And there is [another type of fellow] who yokes [his father] to millstones, yet [despite mistreating his father in this way] receives the Garden of Eden as his inheritance.

How could one who feeds his father fattened [animals, thereby treating him with the utmost respect], receive Gehenna as his inheritance?

A person used to feed his father fat chickens. One time, [fearing that his son might have misappropriated chickens set aside for sacrificial use], his father said to him, "Son, where did you get these [fine birds]?" [His son] said to him, "Old man, old man! Eat and don't complain [about the food], just like dogs that eat [whatever is before them] and never complain!" [Such a person] turns out to feed his father fattened [animals], yet to receive Gehenna as his inheritance.

How could one who yokes his father to the millstones, [thereby mistreating him], receive the Garden of Eden as his inheritance?

A person was grinding at the millstones. When the command came [for one member of each household] to grind [at the royal mill, in service of the King, the son] said to [his father], "Dad, you take up the yoke here in my place, [and I shall go take up the more severe work of grinding for the King]. [In this way], should we [at the royal mill] come to dishonor, it will be better for me—me and not you—[to be dishonored]; should we [at the royal mill] receive lashes, it will be better for me—me and not you—[to receive them]." [Such a person] turns out to yoke his father to the millstones yet receive the Garden of Eden as his inheritance.[12]

The world of discourse for the rabbis who created these matched narratives is imperial Roman society, the culture that the rabbis themselves had to confront. Here we find ordinary folk pressed into royal service; a well-meaning but none too bright, poverty stricken son provides his father with stolen Temple animals he could not possibly afford.

---

12. For a parallel passage, see B. Qiddushin 31a.

And this passage provides us with interesting data, as the rabbis attempted to spell out, finally, the proper course of action. After all, their point was that true respect for parents might be found, paradoxically, in profoundly disrespectful behavior. Children therefore must consider their intention for action, and suit their deeds to achieving that aim. The rabbis' pair of hypothetical narratives, which established legal precedent based on the relationship of sons and fathers, show the potential folly of formal compliance with the law: if one's intent was not to further the spirit of the Fifth Utterance, the law in fact might be abrogated.

In making such assertions, the rabbis of course pick up themes latent in the biblical narratives. Joseph, for instance, treated his father with the greatest disregard, allowing him to suffer in the mistaken belief that his favorite son had died, torn apart by desert beasts (see Gen. 37–47, esp. 42:35–38). From his office as vizier over all Egypt, Joseph easily could have sent word of his well-being. Yet all this was for a more profound respect of father: the deception allowed Joseph to protect his father and family in years of famine. Similarly, the rabbis' tale of Abraham destroying his father's idols makes a similar point (Genesis Rabbah Parashah 38; Gen. 11:28). Such destruction of property ordinarily would constitute profound disrespect for one's parents. Yet in this case, Abraham acted out of love and ultimately respect for his father's spiritual development. The authors of the current Talmudic passage preferred, nonetheless, to draw their precedents from their own spheres of influence and daily lives. Scripture's tales, despite the authority attached to them by reason of revelation, were not to be promoted above freshly created narrative.

Summary

So far as the specifics of how one ought to show respect for parents, the three sets of stories presented thus far simply underscore our existing understanding. Honor ought to be unlimited, of course, a point perfectly clear from the Mishnah itself;

and the rewards paid out to respectful children—again simply parroting the Mishnah's assertion—are received both immediately and in the afterlife. Talmudic expansion along these lines served not to innovate, but merely to reinforce these beliefs.

But attention to the larger structure of this essay on moral exemplars shows the Talmud's material to be rich in meaning. These carefully constructed narratives focused on the activities of a full range of individuals, including gentiles, sages, and ordinary folk. The rabbis took a casuistic approach, thoughtfully arranging the stories at hand so as to draw the student inexorably toward the desired conclusions. The triplet of stories about Dama ben Natina first showed the unlimited extent of one's duty as well as God's fervent desire to reward proper behavior. Then the two sets of matched stories (Rabbi Ishmael and Rabbi Ṭarfon; the paradise-bound, "dishonorable" child, as against the hell-bound, but "respectful," son) together pointed the reader in the direction of intention and its result in action. Thus the rabbis claimed that capricious and sometimes even paradoxical action is required by law—if the broader intention and duty of fulfilling one of the Ten Utterances is thereby realized.

All in all, for the rabbis, personal morality lay in concrete results. What have you accomplished? How has your life turned out? These sorts of questions provided the rabbis with an appropriate ethical standard. Much less important, both here and in general, were mere intentions that never resulted in action,[13] or cultivation of personal attitudes of virtue, unless, of course, these led to proper behavior.

In making these initial assertions about the authority of Jewish law, the rabbis tended to look beyond Scripture. At the outset, as far as the rabbis were concerned, "The Bible tells you so" was not nearly so effective an exhortation as "Here, let me

---

13. See Eilberg-Schwartz, *The Human Will in Judaism,* which treats intention largely as explicative of actions, not as an independent ethical entity. See esp. pp. 13–14 and 137–38.

show you how. . . . " So it is that a simple query about the extent of one's obligations under the law is answered by no less than eight illustrative stories, in which biblical materials played a small role.

Scriptural Authority and Rabbinism

We must not forget that in some contexts, Scripture stood at the head of the hierarchy of authority. Oftentimes entire passages of Talmud were built upon a sophisticated reading of biblical verses, contrasting one formulation with another, explicating this ruling in terms of that biblical phrase. In such contexts, the Hebrew Bible contributed more than just relevant facts and was deemed a repository of truth. These words, spoken and recorded in just this way, captured the thoughts of the living God.[14] They constituted the most accurate reflection the rabbis knew of the world in which they lived. Reality existed in the holy words; the physical realm, for the rabbis, served as a commentary upon, and explanation of, biblical reality.

The Order of Creation

In developing the legal process, then, the rabbis sometimes turned to the lessons one might learn by examining nature: animals, humans, and the cosmos itself all share in being God's creations, and so all might reveal the holiness inherent in the Creator's work.

Think back to the stories about Dama ben Natina. At the outset of the entire Talmudic essay on parental respect, the opening paradigm was the gentile, idol-worshipping head of the city council of Ashkelon. The Talmudic authors implied that

---

14. In at least this sense, Scripture may be seen as a repository of authoritarian norms. See Little and Twiss, *Comparative Religious Ethics*, p. 103.

even a gentile, never commanded by God to honor parents, never the recipient of Sinaitic revelation, knew perfectly well how to follow the divine law! All humans, as children beholden to their parents, should be aware of proper respect. In referring to Dama ben Natina, the rabbis inductively determined the appropriate law; by looking at how people live their lives and at how the world is constructed, we, too, may reason out principles to guide our actions.

A fuller example of the discovery of God's law in the structure of creation is found in the next portion of the essay on respect for parents. Here, the rabbis attempted to compare the respectful attitude commanded toward one's parents with the worshipful attitude Jews hold toward God.

Yerushalmi Peah 1:1 (continued)

It is stated [in Scripture], *"Each person shall revere his mother and father"* (Lev. 19:3). And it [also] is stated [in Scripture], *"Revere only the LORD your God and worship him alone"* (Deut. 6:13).

[By using the word "revere" in both contexts, these verses] compare the reverence one must display toward his father and mother to the reverence he must have for [God in] Heaven.

[Two further comparisons between honoring one's parents and honoring God may be made on the basis of the following verses:] It is stated [in Scripture], *"Honor your father and mother"* (Exod. 20:12). And it [also] is stated [in Scripture], *"Honor the LORD with all your wealth"* (Prov. 3:9). [By using the word "honor" in both contexts, these verses] compare the honor one must display toward his father and mother to the honor one must show the Omnipresent.

It is stated [in Scripture], *"He who curses his father or his mother shall be put to death"* (Exod. 21:17). And it [also] is stated [in Scripture], *"Anyone who curses his God shall bear his guilt"* (Lev. 24:15).

[By using the word "curse" in both contexts, these verses] compare the case of cursing one's father and mother to the case of cursing the Omnipresent.

[The Talmud now raises an objection to the notion that cursing one's parents and cursing God are analogous concepts, based on the context surrounding Exod. 21:17, just cited. That context is a discussion of punishments deserved for striking various individuals, including one's parents (see Exod. 21:15).] But it is not possible [to say] that one might "strike" heaven!

[Despite the foregoing objection, equating God with mother and father] is in accord with strict logic, for all three share [equally in a child's creation].[15]

In this unit, the Talmud examined linguistic parallels found in three sets of verses, and on that basis compared revering, honoring, and cursing one's parents and God. This rhetorical structure, called g^əzerah shavah (equivalence of expression), asserts that Scripture's formulation itself reveals details about a diverse range of concerns, not just about the issues on the surface of the narrative. If the Bible utilized a single word in two separate contexts, then we may equate the two contexts for legal purposes. In the case at hand, however, a problem materialized. Attention to the context surrounding one of the "cursing" verses might lead the reader to abandon the entire comparison between parents and God. This is because it would be entirely inappropriate to describe a person's "striking" heaven as one might slap a parent.

It is instructive to look back at how this problem resolved itself: "[Equating God with mother and father] is in accord with strict logic, for all three share [equally in a child's creation]." The equation of parents and God in the final analysis may be vindicated by appeal to rabbinic reproductive "science," summed up in the following passage.

Bavli Niddah 31a

There are three partners in man. . . . His father supplies the semen of the white substance out of which are formed the child's bones, sinews, nails, brain, and the white in his eye. His mother supplies the semen of the red substance, out of which is formed his skin, flesh, hair, and black of his eye. God gives him the soul and breath, beauty of features, eyesight, hearing, speech, understanding, and discern-

---

15. For a parallel passage, see B. Qiddushin 30b.

ment. When his time comes to depart this world, God takes his share and leaves the shares of his mother and father with them.[16]

The rabbis here invoked the very structure of creation to show that God and parents cooperate in a child's conception. Since all three are "parents," the rabbis asserted, the respect due to all is equal. That is why Scripture compared parents and God through its use of equivalence of expression. The everyday, physical world (as understood by the rabbis) explains the law, and gives the proper understanding of revealed truth.

Reason and Revelation

Yet if the world is a suitable commentary upon Scripture, that alone cannot suffice. Sometimes there arise simple quandaries of everyday life, and these require resolution. For the rabbis, the key to such dilemmas resided in the rabbinic ability to reason logically, usually about the written Word of God. The two sources of truth about the world—the one revealed in God's words, the other revealed in the world about us—thus complemented one another, together pointing out the fullness of God's message.

In the next portion of the Talmudic essay on parental honor, the explicit issue is a son's role in supporting his elderly father. Should he serve merely as administrator of his father's assets, writing checks from Dad's account in order to assure his well-being? Or does the son's filial duty extend further, so that the son himself must purchase all necessities from his own money?

Yerushalmi Peah 1:1 (continued)

What suffices as reverence [of one's father]? One should neither sit in his seat nor speak in his stead, and one should not contradict him.

What suffices as honor [of one's father]? *One should feed him, give him drink, clothe him and give him shoes, take him in and out [at his whim, and wash his face, hands, and feet]* (T. Qid. 1:11B).

---

16. The translation is taken from Feldman, *Marital Relations*, pp. 132–33.

Whose property [must be used in clothing and feeding the father]? [Must the son provide the sustenance from his own resources?] Huna bar Ḥiyya said, "That of the old man [i.e., the father's]." But there are some who wish to say, "His own [i.e., the son must provide what is necessary to support his father]."

[And did] not R. Abbahu affirm this point [that the son bears unlimited responsibility for supporting his father]? [For R. Abbahu said] in the name of R. Yose ben Ḥanina, "How do we know that even if his father said to him, 'Throw that wallet [of yours] into the sea' that [the son] must obey? [He must do so] because [even though] this action causes him distress, it makes his father happy." [The point, contrary to Huna bar Ḥiyya's view, is that the son must do anything or spend any amount in order to make his father happy. . . .]

. . . The [following] opinion of R. Ḥiyya bar Vah disputes [that of R. Huna bar Ḥiyya, who claims that one's responsibility to honor his father extends only to using the father's property]. For [R. Ḥiyya bar Vah] said, "R. Yudan, son of Dorotai taught [in the name] of R. Simeon ben Yoḥai. For he taught: R. Simeon ben Yoḥai says, 'Great is the honor owed to one's father and mother, for the Holy, Blessed One prefers it even to his own honor.'

"[How do we know that God prefers the honoring of one's father and mother to God's own?] It is stated [in Scripture], 'Honor your father and your mother, [that you may long endure on the Land that the LORD your God is assigning you]' (Exod. 20:12), and it [also] is stated [in Scripture], 'Honor the LORD with your wealth, [with the best of all your income]' (Prov. 3:9).

"From what [property should you] honor [God]? From that which sustains you—[thus] one must separate gleanings, forgotten sheaves, and the corner offering; he must separate heave offering, first tithe, second tithe, poor man's tithe and the ḥallah offering; one must make a sukkah, lulav, shofar, phylacteries, and fringes; one must provide food for the poor and the hungry; and one must provide drink for the thirsty. Now if you have any of these items [of food and drink, etc.], you are obligated to [use them in order to honor God] in each and every way [listed]. But if you have nothing, you are not obligated for any one [of them].

"But when one comes to the matter of honoring father and mother, whether or not he has substance, [Scripture still states], 'Honor your father and your mother,' even if [this means that] you must make the rounds, [begging for the wherewithal to honor your parents]." [The point of this long argument is that, in contrast to Huna bar Ḥiyya, Ḥiyya bar Vah thinks that honoring one's parents is so important a duty that one must use all of his property in support of his parents, even in this means that he will become a pauper.]

The brief definitions of "revering" and "honoring" one's parents introduce the Talmud's real interest in this unit, namely, adjudicating between the alternative notions that a child is obligated to use only his father's own estate in supporting him as an old man, or that one must use whatever resources are available, even one's own. The Talmud's attempt to prove (on the basis of Scripture's formulation) that even a child's resources must be utilized in support of aged parents forms the mirror image of the previous section, in which reason and facts about the world resolved a scriptural conundrum. Here the rabbis opened with an appeal to reason: Rabbi Abbahu staked out the stringent option, citing teleological arguments in favor of doing anything to gladden one's parents. Huna bar Ḥiyya took the opposite view. The question finally was settled only through recourse to Scripture's wording, in an argument *a minori ad majus*. One must "honor" both God and parents, but since Scripture left the commandment regarding parents so abstract, even the use of the children's resources (in addition to the parents' estate) is mandated. The Talmud's authors deduced the appropriate law for everyday life from the quintessential piece of creation, the Bible. Its character (i.e., linguistic formulation) not only captured God's revelation, but served to explain the duty of ordinary folk in their daily interactions with parents.

Discovering the Spirit of the Law

As the essay on the Fifth Utterance continues and finally comes to a close, the rabbis note that Scripture's language suggests an equation between a most serious matter—respecting parents—and a trivial command—sending forth a mother bird before taking her chicks (Deut. 22:6). In asking why the Hebrew Bible would compare these commands, the rabbinic authors grounded human reason in the biblical materials, showing that, in the spirit of halakhic inquiry, only an integrated vision of the whole of Judaic theology will suffice.

Yerushalmi Peah 1:1 (continued)

. . . Said R. Ba bar Kahana, "Scripture compares the least of all religious duties to the most weighty of all, [in order to show that one must perform all of the commandments]. [What is] the least of all [religious duties specified in the Torah]? That would be sending forth the mother hen [while you take care of the chicks] (Deut. 22:6). And the most weighty? That would be honoring one's father and mother. Now with regard to both of these [religious duties, the same reward] is written [in Scripture], ' . . . that you may long endure [in the land.] . . .'"

Said R. Avun, "[Scripture compares sending forth the mother hen to honoring one's parents not because they are equally weighty, but for the following reason:] If with regard to a matter that is tantamount to a repayment of a debt [i.e., honoring one's parents, who bore, raised, and educated one], it is written [in Scripture], ' . . . that you may long endure, and that you may fare well, in the land that the LORD your God is assigning to you' (Deut. 5:16), with regard to a matter that involves a loss of money and mortal danger [i.e., by sending forth the mother hen, one loses the value of the bird and is in danger of falling out of the tree], how much more so [does the reward of long life apply, as stated at Deut. 22:7]."

Said R. Levi—and this is the opinion of the rabbis—"[Honoring one's parents is deemed more important than sending forth the mother hen, because in general] a matter involving the repayment of a debt is deemed more important than something that does not involve repayment of a debt."

R. Simeon ben Yohai taught, "Just as the reward [for performing these two religious duties] is equivalent, so, too, the punishment [for failure to perform them] is equivalent."

What reasoning [allows him to derive this point from Scripture]? [Consider the following exegesis offered for Prov. 30:17:] "The eye that mocks a father and disdains the homage due a mother—[the ravens of the brook will gouge it out, young eagles will devour it]." "The eye that mocks [a father] . . . " has ridiculed the notion of honoring one's father and mother, and [the eye] that " . . . *disdains the homage due [a mother]* . . . " refers to not taking the mother hen with her chicks. [Since this verse is construed to refer to both commandments, the single punishment specified, having one's eyes picked out, must be the same for failure to perform the two duties.]

The rabbis wished to assert that all commandments, from large to small, must be scrupulously followed. Here they follow a general principle of duty, found in an explicit command of Scripture ("Gather the people . . . that they may learn . . . to observe every word of this Teaching [*torah*]" [Deut. 31:12]). But in following Scripture's lead, Rabbi Avun and Rabbi Levi sought rational arguments to explain the parallel language in Scripture applied to honoring parents and sending forth the mother hen. To this end, they first consider the danger involved in following each command; and second, they heed the seriousness of the debt one owes to one's parents.

In other words, since the reward specified in Scripture for honoring parents was the same as that for sending forth a mother hen, the rabbis asserted that God, in so writing the two verses, had made a broader point that well-applied reason could ferret out: one must perform all of the commandments, whether large or small, and doing so earns the reward of long life.

Summary

God's revelation in Word and in the World are neatly related and intertwined. For its part, Scripture grounds the human intellect as it observes God's creation, providing a clear framework. All that people observe in everyday life and thought— the moral principles they derive and the particular laws they deduce—exist within the realm of choices laid out in the Bible. The Holy Word allowed the rabbis to understand the world about them. At the same time, and correlatively, the physical world, together with the logic inherent in humanity, might explain God's revelation.

Seeking Scripture's Spirit Beyond Its Letter

The principles of scriptural interpretation we have just seen—in particular, the integration of the Hebrew Bible and rabbinic tradition, and the requirement to carry out the purposes of the law, sometimes even through paradoxical actions—show themselves in other contexts. For example, at times the rabbis, taking a longer view of the consequences of enforcing Scripture's laws and punishments, found it necessary to act upon their own authority and to legislate so as to uphold the spirit, but not the plain meaning, of a rule.

This rabbinic assertion of authority took place most commonly in determinations of punishments for violating Scripture's rules. In each of the following two brief passages, a rabbinic court reduced the Bible's specified punishment for violating one of the Ten Utterances.

Mishnah Makkot 1:3

[If people testified], "We testify that so and so is subject to receive flogging in the measure of forty stripes," but they turn out to be perjurers—

"They themselves receive eighty stripes: [forty] on the count of *'You shall not bear false witness against your neighbor'* (Exod. 20:13), and [forty] on the count of *'You shall do to him as he schemed to do to his fellow'* (Deut. 19:19)," the words of R. Meir.

But sages say, "They are flogged only forty stripes."

No explanation here is given for the sages' diminishing the perjurer's punishment, but the rationale seems straightforward. Eighty lashes seems too extreme a punishment—well nigh a capital punishment—for a single action on the part of the perjured witness. Rather than allow perjurers to receive overly stiff penalties, the sages inflicted more lenient punishment than called for by the two appropriate verses. In so doing, the rabbis chose not to act upon Scripture's careful—and in R. Meir's opinion—purposive replication. Instead, they act in accord with the underlying principle of Deut. 25:3, "He may be given up to forty lashes, but not more, lest being flogged further, your brother be degraded before your eyes." In light of this verse, the sages chose to enforce the law in a manner that preserves human dignity, even that of a criminal.

A slightly more explicit example regards violation of the Third Commandment. Since a false oath may cause irreparable damage to a transgressor's hope for eventual redemption, the sages again asserted themselves within the legal system.

Yerushalmi Shevuot 3:10 [Venice: 35a; Vilna: 18b]

[The penalty owing to one who makes a false oath is specified in] the following general rule:

[Violation of] any negative commandment whose observance involves an actual deed is punished by flogging, but [violation of] any negative commandment whose observance does not involve a concrete deed is not punished by flogging; except for (1) one who verbally [substitutes an unconsecrated animal for one already sanctified] (cf. Lev. 27:10); (2) one who takes a [false] oath; and (3) one who curses his fellow using [God's] Holy Name.

R. Abbahu in the name of R. Yohanan: "One who verbally [substitutes one animal for another] does not belong [on this list], for verbal substitution involves *both* a statement and an action."

One who takes a false oath—how do we know [that he is to be flogged, but not held irredeemably guilty]? R. Yohanan in the name of R. Yannai: "'[You shall not swear falsely by the name of the LORD your God;] for the LORD will not clear one who swears falsely by [the LORD's] name' (Exod. 20:7). [Scripture specifies only that God will not forgive the transgression], but the judges [for their part] do hold him guiltless [through flogging]. . . . "[17]

Despite the Bible's apparent statement to the contrary, those who abuse God's name are not to be held irredeemably guilty. Instead, they take their lumps and are forgiven fully by rabbinic judges. This major shift in the coercive authority from God's eternal punishment to the court's flogging and forgiving, rests

---

17. For a parallel passage, see B. Temurah 3a–b.

in a detail of Scripture itself (which specifies only that *God* will not forgive perjurers). As enforcers of God's law, the judges, for their part, determined that the consequences attendant upon strict punishment would be too severe. So, by imposing its own punishments, the court sets the stage for God's forbearance. Instead of the extreme punishment of *karet* (extirpation; being "cut off" from the divine and from the world to come), the rabbis here followed the broader, life-promoting spirit of Jewish law—"You shall keep My laws and My rules, by the pursuit of which man shall live" (Lev. 18:5, Ezek. 20:11, 13, 21)—and so attempt to assuage the stringent penalty.

The Effects of Force Majeur

As the authoritative enforcer of Jewish law, rabbinic courts also found legal means to relax biblical definitions of transgression, when strict adherence would run counter to the clear principles underlying the biblical material. Take, for example, the case that arises if the imperial government forces Jews to transgress rabbinic law, perhaps by violating the Sabbath. The rabbis would be met with a dilemma. On the one hand, they might reason absolutely: by definition the only proper course of action is to follow Sabbath law. State enforced punishment for ignoring the imperial decree would be a regrettable, but unavoidable, consequence of loyalty to God and Torah.

On the other hand, the rabbis might resolve the conflict by once again considering that Jewish law seeks the preservation and promotion of life. Rather than allow imperial punishment against Jews who refuse to knuckle under to the state's exertion of *force majeur*, the rabbis might define such action not to be "transgression." Such "sinners" would be held innocent, having acted only under coercive duress.

The following unit presents just such a predicament, now related to rabbinic evidentiary standards and violation of both the Sabbatical year (cf. Lev. 25:1–7) and the Sabbath itself. At issue in the Mishnah passage that occasions the Talmud's inquiry is whether someone who transgresses Jewish law remains competent to serve as a witness in a rabbinic court.

Mishnah Sanhedrin 3:3

The following are incompetent [to serve as witnesses or judges]: (1) one who plays dice, (2) one who loans money on interest, (3) those who race pigeons, and (4) those who do business in the produce of the Sabbatical year.

Said R. Simeon, "In the beginning they called them 'Those who gather Sabbatical year produce.' But when oppressors [who collected taxes in the Sabbatical year] multiplied, they resorted to calling them 'Those who do business in the produce of the Sabbatical year.'"

Said R. Judah, "Under what circumstances [are those who deal in Sabbatical year produce incompetent]? When they have only that as their profession. But if they have a profession other than that, they are competent."

Jacob Neusner sums up the crux of the issue to be addressed by the Talmud:

A fresh and interesting question follows. It is whether we are to distinguish diverse causes for violating the law. The trend of the discussion is to distinguish, in particular, the state's forcing Jews to violate the Torah essentially for reasons neutral to Judaism, e.g., the state's own service or convenience, and Jews being forced to apostatize and so violate the law and so to disgrace God and the Torah. It is this latter kind of pressure, but not the former, which Jews must resist at all costs. . . . [18]

The Talmudic passage, which follows, has been broken into smaller segments for comment. Its direct reference to the Ten Utterances occurs in several of the middle segments, regarding forced violation of the Sabbath, and, at the end, dealing with vain uses of God's name.

---

18. Neusner, *The Talmud of the Land of Israel*, vol. 31, *Tractate Sanhedrin*, pp. 110-11.

Yerushalmi Sanhedrin 3:3 [Venice: 21a–b; Vilna: 15b–17a]

. . . What would be a concrete example [of Judah's position that those whose sole business is trade in Sabbatical year produce are incompetent to serve as witnesses, despite the secular government's oppressive taxation]?

One who sits idle during the other [six years] of the Sabbatical cycle. But once the Sabbatical year arrives, he sets out to do business in produce of the Sabbatical year (T. San. 5:2). So if he has yet another profession, he is competent; if not he is incompetent [to serve as a witness or judge].

Now if one carried out his own profession throughout all the years of the Sabbatical cycle, and if, once the Sabbatical year arrives, he sets out instead to do business in produce of the Sabbatical year, even though such a person has no other profession [in the Sabbatical year itself], he [too] is competent.

R. Ba bar Zaveda, R. Abbahu in the name of R. Eleazar: "The law accords with R. Judah's opinion in the Mishnah [M. San. 3:3]." R. Ba bar Zabeda was praised because he stated this tradition in the name of someone [Abbahu] who was younger than he. . . .

Here the rabbis formulated their basic question of standards of competency to serve as a witness. The Talmud's main point was that ordinary working folk, in the normal course of life under imperial rule, may have to deal in Sabbatical year produce to pay taxes. Such people should not incur negative consequences in a court. By contrast, those who seek to profit because of the government's interference—making their living solely off of the sale of ordinarily forbidden fruit—clearly ought to receive no protection from the full wrath of rabbinic law. The general principle established here is now addressed in the remainder of the unit through several stories and individual applications.

Yerushalmi Sanhedrin 3:3 (continued)

. . . When the government first became oppressive, R. Yannai gave instructions that the people might plough once only [during the Sabbatical year, thus minimizing the extent to which they worked the land during that year]. An apostate to idolatry—a transgressor of the laws of the Sabbatical year—saw people breaking up the large clods of earth, and said, "What perversion! You were granted permission to plough, [so as to comply with the government's tax edict], but not to break up the ploughed clods!"

Said R. Jacob bar Zavedi, "I once asked R. Abbahu, 'Didn't Zeira and R. Yoḥanan say in the name of R. Yannai, [or] R. Yoḥanan in the name of R. Simeon b. Yehoṣedeq: "They voted in the upper room of the house of Nitzeh in Lydda: 'In regard to the Torah, how do we know that, if an idolator should force an Israelite to transgress one of the religious duties stated in the Torah, the [Israelite] should do so without incurring the death penalty, with the exception of idolatry, fornication, and murder? [Scripture states, *"You shall keep My laws and My rules, by the pursuit of which man shall live"* (Lev. 18:5)]' [19]—Now that rule applies to transgressions in private; but if the transgression would be in public, one must not obey the idolator and transgress even the most trivial prohibition." Illustrating this point, there is the case of Papus and Lulianos, his brother, to whom [idolators] gave water in a colored glass flask. They did not accept the water [because the flask bore an idol's name]. [So how could Yannai have permitted the people to plough in the seventh year?]'"

[Abbahu] said, "[The case of tax payments is different. For the government] does not wish to enforce apostasy, but merely to levy taxes. [In such a case it is permitted publicly to violate the laws of the Torah]. . . ."[20]

Rabbi Yannai makes his rationale—and the rabbis' mode of argument—explicit at the end. In asking Jews to work the land during the Sabbatical year, the Roman government had no intention of enforcing apostasy, but merely wished to collect taxes. Since the state exerts *force majeur*, the Israelites cannot be held guilty, and the rabbis may permit what would otherwise be a public violation of Jewish law. But the rabbis take careful note of the intention and purposes of both the government and the Jewish citizen. One may "violate" Jewish law in this case only because no one—not the Jews, not the government agent—ever intended that act to be a violation.

---

19. For the bracketed material, see B. Sanhedrin 74a.
20. For parallel passages, see B. Sanhedrin 26a–b and 74a–b.

Perhaps of equal interest, however, is the epitome of the Torah's most serious laws, for which even *force majeur* offers no
defense: idolatry, fornication, and murder. These cut to the
heart of the rabbinic system, with its emphasis on holiness in
matters of cult, family, and society: idolators deny God's existence and sole sovereignty, thus destabilizing the Israelite religious world; fornicators and adulterers ignore normal familial
ties, thereby destroying and tearing apart families; and mur-
derers break the most basic social aspects of the covenant, making normal life in community next to impossible. So damaging
are these three sins that, whether in public or private, no matter
what type of duress is applied, a Jew is forbidden to perform
them.

Other, more minor transgressions may be committed under
duress, without incurring liability, so long as the violation does
not set a public precedent. As if once again to highlight the
importance of the intention with which a coerced sin is committed, the rabbis now continue with yet two more illustrations.

Yerushalmi Sanhedrin 3:3 (continued)

. . . R. Yonah and R. Yose gave instructions to bake bread for [the
Roman general] Ursicinus on the Sabbath.

Said R. Mani, "I once asked R. Yonah, 'Father, didn't R. Zeira and
R. Yohanan say in the name of R. Yannai, [or] R. Jeremiah, R. Yohanan
in the name of R. Simeon b. Yehosedeq: "They voted in the upper room
of the house of Nitzeh [to the effect that public transgression must
never be sanctioned]"? [So how can you permit Jews to bake bread in
public on the Sabbath?]'"

[R. Yonah answered], "[The rabbis] did not intend to enforce apostasy, but rather to allow him to eat warm bread. . . . "

. . . R. Ba bar Zamina used to sew clothes for a Roman. [His em-
ployer] brought him carrion meat and told him to eat. [R. Ba] replied,
"I won't eat that." [The Roman] said, "Eat, or I'll kill you." [R. Ba]
replied, "If you want to kill me, go ahead; but I'm not going to eat
carrion meat." [The Roman] said to him, "Who told you [that my intention was to test you]? Had you eaten the meat, I would have killed

you. If you are going to be a Jew, be a Jew. If you are going to be a Roman, be a Roman."

Said R. Mana, "Had R. Ba bar Zamina heard the teaching of the rabbis, [who said that it is all right to transgress in private,] he would have eaten in this case!"

These two episodes raise a basic question: even if allowed by rabbinic decree to violate a commandment, should Jews act in such a manner? Rabbi Ba bar Zamina set a high standard when he refused to eat unsuitable food even at the risk of his own life. Ordinarily, in line with the decree cited earlier, a Jew would be permitted to eat, rather than forfeit longevity. Yet the inculcation of attributes of holiness may lead one to act above and beyond the call of the law; this, too, is praiseworthy—and, in the case at hand, good political sense. The Roman employer sums things up tidily: "If you are going to be a Jew, be a Jew. If you are going to be a Roman, be a Roman."

The finale to this long passage again asks whether the rabbinic relaxation of Jewish law is valid and wise. After a few quick examples of this sort of rabbinic laxity, Rabbi Yose bar Rabbi Bun invokes the issue of fidelity to the one God, and delineates those areas in which absolute submission to Jewish law is required.

Yerushalmi Sanhedrin 3:3 (continued)

. . . When [the Roman general] Proclus came to Sepphoris, R. Mana instructed the bakers to put out [bread] in the marketplace [on the Sabbath]; [under similar circumstances], the rabbis of Naveh gave instructions [to the bakers] to bake leavened bread on Passover.

Said R. Yose b. R. Bun, "'[Who knows the meaning of the adage: "A man's wisdom lights up his face, so that his deep discontent is dissembled"?] I do! "Obey the king's orders—and don't rush into uttering an oath by God."' (Eccles. 8:1–2)—the command of the King of Kings do I keep, who said to me at Sinai, 'I the LORD am your God' (Exod. 20:2). [Ecclesiastes' juxtaposition of 'the king's orders' and 'an oath by God' implies that] the commandment, 'You shall have no other gods besides Me' (Exod. 20:3) refers only to the oath of God, [as in a following verse]: 'You shall not swear falsely by the name of the LORD your God' (Exod. 20:7)."

[Proper relations to the ruling government may also be derived from King Nebuchadnezzar's name]: In all other matters (Hebrew: kadevar hazeh, like [Nevu]khadnezzar) you rule (Hebrew: nevu, as if he was a prophet, navi)—[this implies taxes and corvées]. But in the matter of [divine oaths], that man and a dog are equal [to us, for we obey neither].

R. Judah in the name of Rav: "The law accords with R. Judah."

At the outset, note the final ruling of Rav: the Mishnaic law (upon which all discussion here has been based) accords with the opinion of Rabbi Judah. People who transgress the law only to satisfy tax bills should remain innocent. Confronted with circumstances outside of their control, the rabbis focused their legal procedure upon the intention with which an act was performed. And in the main, minor violations of the law could be countenanced when the intent was promotion of good relations with the imperial government. Rabbi Yose made a similar claim: when the state wishes to interfere, one ought to render unto Caesar what is Caesar's. Tax bills must be paid, one way or another. Doing so is not sinful, but a necessary accommodation to life under non-Jewish rulers.

But such secular payments are as far as the matter goes. If ever an act demanded by the needs of statecraft were to involve even the slightest diminution of the exclusive respect demanded by God, Rabbi Yose ruled, it would be utterly forbidden as a violation of the First Utterance. Thus, the imperial king, here represented typologically by Nebuchadnezzar, cannot command perfect loyalty: one must not elevate the king to semidivine status by taking secular oaths, anymore than one would use a dog's name to seal an important vow. Any other attitude here would involve a direct violation of the Second Utterance, for the person would have taken a god other than the King of Kings, blessed be God. Of course, in more straightforwardly secular matters, the secular king rules. In all such cases, the implication is that the rabbis' relaxation of Torah rules holds.

Summary

All in all, the rabbis asserted the right to determine when the Torah's rules should and should not apply. Their determinations stand in sharp contrast to a notion of absolute liability. In the Written Torah, for example, violation of a law or regulation immediately implies one's guilt, without respect to circumstance or one's intentions. And insofar as it contained the prima facie norms that guide the community, Scripture was the first authority consulted by the rabbis. Yet the Talmud's authors held circumstance and intentions paramount. The court, as the body applying Jewish law, had to make life under the law bearable and possible. Court consideration of the consequences attendant upon strictly enforcing the law, and of the intentions with which actions were performed, was a necessary component in the humanization of the law and its ethical application.

Rabbinic Ethics and Authority

Rabbinic Judaism portrays itself as a religion of the Word. The Written Torah stands at the top of rabbinism's hierarchy of authority, capturing forever the divine commands. Jews in this scheme are, as I have indicated, the people of the Book, which is to be read carefully and lovingly. In no small measure, this affinity for Scripture's words has contributed to the depiction of literalistic, legalistic Judaism so pervasive throughout history. "Judaism is the religion of the Old Testament"—emphasis on *Old*, emphasis on the static, inflexible, harsh, legal *Testament*.

But the Bible turns out to have a different place in moral argument than we might have thought. Rarely did the Talmud invoke an authoritarian validation for the Ten Utterances. Such justifications as "because the Bible tells me so . . . " do not appear often in the materials we have surveyed; almost always, such appeals appear within a structured discourse whose point transcends the fundamentalistic tendency. The Bible indeed was a source of authority, but not the only such source in the challenging and unclear world of Talmudic discourse.

How then was the Bible utilized, and why was it so prized in Jewish self-depictions? The answer, I think, involves the rabbinic theological melding of the categories of creation and revelation. On the one hand, God's creatures and creations act within an ordered sphere, which itself reveals norms and action—guides for humanity. Through creating the physical world and in directing human logic and intellection, God has expressed a revelation coordinated with, but separate from, the Written Torah. So the Written Torah (that is, the Bible) looms large when the rabbis wish to adjudicate disputes and dilemmas. Even more, appeals to the Bible show the integrity of all God's actions, both creative and revelatory. For the rabbis, truth is found both in the Word of God and in God's world.

Alongside such coordination of biblical texts and the whole of creation, the halakhic process employs personal stories about rabbis and common folk to exemplify proper behavior. By using moral paradigms, the rabbis move beyond mere statements of law, again rejecting simple authoritarianism. In its place, the rabbis orient their thought toward the goals, purposes, and results of the law. Biblical law ought to be upheld, at the simplest level, because this brings about the best consequences: the rabbis were well aware that God rewards law-abiding subjects, while meting out punishment upon those who disobey. It is a simple matter, therefore, to reason one's way to following God's Ten Utterances and the entire legal corpus.

Rabbinic law itself, however, develops and refines the biblical legislation, and in so doing draws the astute student away from mere consequentialism to a deeper pursuit of holiness in action. How, for example, should one honor mother and father? The rabbis painstaking spell out the implications of biblical Commandments in their many rules and stories. Fulfilling rabbinic law is a matter of acting with the proper frame of mind, of accomplishing an overarching goal. People honor their parents (and observe all of God's commands) in order to receive rewards; but meritorious action is defined by a person's intention. This attention to one's purposes in acting applies to determining the law both on the personal level and through court decisions. An individual might well have to act paradoxically in order to carry out the aims of halakhic mandates; similarly, if enforcing the law stringently would evade the purposes of the legal system, courts find legal means to enforce the spirit of the revelation at Sinai.

By articulating the rationale behind observance of the Ten Utterances, the rabbis exemplify their integrated ethical system: God's Commandments are an absolute authority, demanding observance by mere definition. Whenever possible, the formulation of Scripture thus determines the law's application. But rabbinic moral theology seeks further clarification, holding paramount always the dual effects of purpose and consequence. What end is intended by biblical legislation? What consequences will follow upon action? These considerations flesh out the biblical injunctions, allowing the rabbinic legal process the flexibility that was its characteristic up to modern times. It is this multifaceted approach to the law that promotes the ultimate goal of rabbinism, found so stunningly in the First Utterance: "I the LORD am your God who brought you out of the land of Egypt, the house of bondage." *Halakhah* thus adjures one to the life of holiness, found in absolute submission to God, exclusive respect for God's actions in history, and always expressed through the letter—and the spirit—of biblical law.

6. The Spirit of Rabbinic Law

The Rabbinization of Revelation

In developing halakhic materials based on the Ten Utterances, the rabbis saw themselves as effecting a return, in legal theory, to the heart of the Sinaitic revelation. Their foundational theological assertions regarding the unified character of the Oral and Written Law and the authority that undergirded their own efforts stem from a single implicit assertion: the rabbinic consistory constituted the one and only authentic interpretive community, which, participating in the processes of Jewish law, could both innovate and, at the same time, conserve the tradition.

The rabbis of the Talmud of the Land of Israel thus deemed the Ten Utterances fundamental to Jewish theology, asserting that the central prayer of Jewish liturgy—the *Shema* that proclaims God's oneness—indirectly referred to each Commandment in turn. So even if the Ten Utterances as a larger whole were never construed as a précis of the Bible's law, and even if the rabbis preferred other biblical passages as the basis for their discussions of various laws, still they recognized the foundational character of the biblical construct, representing the entirety of God's revelation on Mount Sinai.

The attempts to coordinate the rules of the Ten Utterances with theological principles the rabbis held independently to define Judaism did not (and does not) slavishly adhere to the letter of the received law. Judaism as a whole ignores that kind of literalism, in favor rather of developing other topics of far greater weight and importance. Rabbinic attitudes toward the individual Utterances likewise reflect this tendency to develop connections merely implicit in Scripture, if obvious to the rabbis. So, for example, we have seen the rabbis equate acts of idolatry with cessation of Torah study. Just as one should be punished for worshipping an idol, so, too, one should be punished for interrupting a life of studying rabbinic literature. This refinement of Jewish theology was far from implicit in the letter of biblical law, but rather emerged from the rabbis' assertion that God's historical relationship to Israel creates a covenantal imperative to understand and follow the whole Torah, for to do any less would be idolatrous. By no means literalists, we found the rabbis, in their detailed study of the individual Commandments, searching always for deeper understandings, for new layers of meaning behind the letter of the law.

As the rabbis sought to appreciate the whole of Jewish law, similarly, they developed an integrated approach to the authority that underlay *halakhah* as a whole. They made common appeal to the moral example set by great rabbis; they based their interpretations on the created order about them, as they saw God's law revealed even in the actions of gentiles, and, of course, in the written words of Scripture. These facts are important because how people justify the rules they adumbrate gives us a powerful indication of what they consider to be of greatest import. And, for the Talmud's authors, the overarching spirit of the Decalogue was the paramount guide to developing the law. When circumstances warranted, the rabbis commuted sentences, even allowed for actions that otherwise would be outside licit bounds. While God's revelation was of greatest import, the rabbis nonetheless had taken for themselves the daunting task of explaining what Sinai meant. If Moses shattered the Tablets, due to the Israelites' infidelity to God even in the face of the stunning redemption from Egyptian bondage, the rabbis gathered those shards of the Stone Tablets that best addressed the world they had to confront. Although never removing their gaze from the wholeness of the Decalogue's message, they included within the Talmud discourses only upon those Utterances that best advanced the return to Sinai.

The Letter and the Spirit

And yet the rabbinic message is more complex than it might at first seem, eschewing finally a selective interpretation of *halakhah* and the Ten Utterances. For if the rabbis did break apart the Decalogue's unity, they also refused to permit this to become the norm.

Yerushalmi Megillah 4:5 [Venice: 75b; Vilna: 31b]

R. Simeon, the scribe of Ţarbenet, [used to read the scrolls in the synagogue service]. The people of his town said to him, "Cut up the Ten Commandments word by word, so that our children may grasp them." He went and asked R. Ḥanina [about this practice]. He replied, "Even if they cut off your head, don't accede to their request." So [R. Simeon] did not obey them, and they dismissed him from the reader's position.

Some time later, he visited Babylonia, and stood with R. Simeon ben Yosinah. So [R. Simeon the scribe] asked [R. Simeon ben Yosinah], "What do you do in your town?" and laid out the entire story. [R. Simeon ben Yosinah] replied, "Why didn't you just follow their request?" [R. Simeon the scribe] responded, "Is such a thing done?" [R. Simeon ben Yosinah] said, "Don't we cut up the portions in the study house?" to which [R. Simeon the scribe] responded, "But don't we also go back and read each verse in its completion?"

Said R. Zeira, "If this scribe had been present [in Babylonia] in my day, I would have appointed him as a sage."

The realization that the study house and the house of worship symbolically represent separate realms has great impact. The rabbis themselves, in developing and editing the Talmudic materials we have reviewed, lived within the study house (or at least within its intellectual framework). Here alone scholars could freely juxtapose one Commandment with another, so as to result in theological principles sometimes no more than implicit in the biblical legal antecedents.

And if the rabbinic treatment of the Ten Utterances resulted in shattering the Tablets, in cutting each Commandment off from its rightful context, that presented no problem. As Simeon the Scribe so eloquently stated, "Don't we also go back and read each verse in its completion?" Rabbinic interpretations of the Ten Utterances—or of any biblical topic—are carried out with an eye to the whole of Jewish law, with appreciation not only of the biblical context, but of the unfolding legal system that binds all Israelites. The true mark of wisdom, for which one earns the title "sage," lies in understanding that the freedom of the rabbinic mind does operate within parameters, and is a product of the study house.

The house of worship, by contrast, would require a different attitude toward God's revelation. The rabbis themselves urged a wholistic understanding of the Sinaitic law. Each Commandment, the Ten Utterances as a whole, together did make a cogent statement: one must keep God and the divine word in the forefront always. Each aspect of God's revelation pointed toward this single theological principle: there is but one God, who commands exclusive worship and proper behavior within creation.

Study of Torah Is Equivalent to All the Commandments

Jewish tradition holds that, like Simeon the Scribe, rabbis have great affection for the careful use of words. They take pains to protect them and render them accurately and communicatively. Throughout this study, the rabbis' concern for God's Word has emerged as paramount: rabbinic law is to be carefully coordinated with the Written Word; the created order, revealed in the cosmos itself, is the counterpart of the Written Word; even if required to make fanciful arguments, the rabbis wish to accord the Written Word ultimate, if not primary, authority.

Mishnah Qiddushin 1:10

Whoever fulfills a single commandment is treated favorably, his days are lengthened, and he inherits the Land [of Israel].

But whoever refrains from a single commandment is treated poorly, his days are not lengthened, and he does not inherit the Land.

Whoever does not have learning in Scripture, Mishnah, and right conduct has no share in society.

But one who clings to all three is referred to by Scripture itself: *"A threefold cord is not readily broken!"* (Eccles. 4:12).

The key to rabbinic theology, then, is the integration of God's revealed Word, found in the Bible itself, with the world of humanity. The Mishnah and Talmud, containing the rabbinic summary and expansion of customary law, were accorded the status of Sinaitic revelation. The halakhic materials, combined with Scripture's laws, together comprised the dual legacy of Judaism: the Written and Oral Torahs, coordinate and complementary, each piece finding its counterpart in the other. The third strand of the rabbinic theological rope—right conduct—here points to the essential ingredient in any legal application: the Jewish sense of right and wrong, which alone allows the law given at Sinai to live from generation to generation.

The Talmudic Texts begin on page 180.

על פני, שבועת אלהים: לא תשא את שם ה' אלהיך לשוא. כדבר
הזה נבוא. ההוא גברא וההן כלבא שניהן שוין. רב יהודה בשם
רב: הלכה כרבי יהודה.

ירושלמי מגילה ד:ה

רבי שמעון ספרא דטרבנת - אמרון ליה בני קרתיה: קטע
בדיביברייא דיקרונון בנינן. אתא שאל לרבי חנינה. אמר ליה:
אין קטעון רישך לא תשמע לון! ולא שמע לון, ושרון ליה מן
ספרוותה. בתר יומין נחת להכא; קם עימיה רבי שמעון בן יוסינה.
אמר ליה: מי את עביד בההוא קרתך, ותני ליה עובדא. אמר ליה:
ולמה לא שמעת לון? אמר ליה: ועבדין כן? אמר ליה: ולינן
מקטעין לון בסידרא? אמר ליה: ולינן חזרין וכללין לון?! אמר רבי
זעירא: אילו הוה ההוא ספרא ביומוי מניתיה חכים.

משנה קידושין א:י

כל העושה מצוה אחת מטיבין לו ומאריכין לו את ימיו ונוחל את
הארץ. וכל שאינו עושה מצוה אחת אין מטיבין לו ואין מאריכין
לו את ימיו ואינו נוחל את הארץ. כל שישנו במקרא ובמשנה
ובדרך ארץ לא במהרה הוא חוטא, שנאמר: והחוט המשלש לא
במהרה ינתק.

דמתניתא. איקלס רבי בא בר זבדא דמר שמועה משום דזעיר
מיניה....

בראשונה כשהיתה המלכות אונסת הורי רבי ינאי שיהו חורשין
חרשה הראשונה. חד מומר לעבודת כוכבים הוה איעבר בשמיטתא
חמתין רמיין קובעתיה. אמר לון: האסטו שרה מרדה; שרא לכון
מירמא קובעת? אמר רבי יעקב בר זבדי קשיתה קומי רבי אבהו:
לא כן אמר זעירא ורבי יוחנן בשם רבי ינאי. רבי ירמיה רבי יוחנן
בשם רבי שמעון בן יהוצדק: נמנו בעליית בית נתזה בלוד: על
התורה מניין אם אמר עובד כוכבים לישראל לעבור על אחת מכל
מצות האמורות בתורה חוץ מעבודת אלילים וגילוי עריות ושפיכות
דמים יעבור ואל ייהרג! הדא דתימר בינו לבין עצמו; אבל ברבים
אפילו על מצוה קלה אל ישמע לו, כגון פפוס ולוליינוס אחיו שנתנו
להן מים בכלי זכוכית צבועה ולא קיבלו מהן. אמר: לא אתכוין
משמדתהון, אלא מגבי ארנונין....

רבי יונה ורבי יוסי הורון למפי לארטיקנס בשובתא. אמר רבי מני
קשיתה קומי רבי יונה אבא: ולא כן אמר רבי זעירא רבי יוחנן
בשם רבי ינאי רבי ירמיה רבי יוחנן בשם רבי שמעון בן יהוצדק:
נמנו בעליית בית נתזה וכו'. לא אתכוין משמדתהון, אלא איתכוון
מיכול פיתא חמימא....

רבי בא בר זימנא הוה מחיט גבי חד בר נש ברומי. אייתי ליה בשר
נבילה, אמר ליה: אכול! אמר ליה: לי נא אכיל. אמר ליה: אכול
דלא כן אנא קטיל לך! אמר ליה. אין בעית מיקטול קטול, דלי נא
אכול בשר נבילה. אמר ליה: מאן מודע לך דאילו אכלתה הוינה
קטלין לך? אי יהודי יהודי אי ארמאי ארמאי. אמר רבי מנא:
אילו הוה רבי בא בר זימנא שמע מיליהון דרבנן מיזל הוה בהדא....
רבי מנא כד עאל פרוקלא בציפורי הורי מפקא נחתומיא בשוקא.
רבנין דנוה הורו מפי חמיע בפיסחא. אמר רבי יוסי בי רבי בון: אני
פי מלך שמור - אני פי מלך מלכי המלכים אשמור, שאמר לי
בסיני: אנכי ה' אלהיך. ועל דברת: לא יהיה לך אלהים אחרים

אכזרי ויקרנה ואל יהנה ממנה. ויאכלוה בני נשר - יבוא נשר
שהוא רחמן ויאכלנה ויהנה ממנה.

משנה מקות א:ג

מעידין אנו באיש פלוני שהוא חייב מלקות ארבעים, ונמצאו
זוממים - לוקין שמונים, משום לא תענה ברעך עד שקר, ומשום
ועשיתם לו כאשר זמם; דברי רבי מאיר. וחכמים אומרים: אינן
לוקין אלא ארבעים.

ירושלמי שבועות ג:י

זה הכלל: כל לא תעשה שיש בו מעשה - לוקה; ושאין בו מעשה -
אינו לוקה, חוץ מן המימר והנשבע ומקלל את חבירו בשם. רבי
אבהו בשם רבי יוחנן לית כאן מימר. מימר דיבור ומעשה נשבע
לשקר מניין? רבי יוחנן בשם רבי ינאי: כי לא ינקה ה'; מנקין הן
הדיינין.

משנה סנהדרין ג:ג

ואלו הן הפסולין: המשחק בקוביא והמלוה ברבית ומפריחי יונים
וסוחרי שביעית. אמר רבי שמעון: בתחלה היו קורין אותן אוספי
שביעית; משרבו האנסין חזרו לקרותן סוחרי שביעית. אמר רבי
יהודה: אימתי? בזמן שאין להם אמנות אלא היא, אבל יש להן
אמנות שלא היא - כשרין.

ירושלמי סנהדרין ג:ג

היך עבידא? יושב ובטל כל שני שבוע, כיון שבאת שביעית התחיל
פושט את ידיו ונושא ונותן בפירות שביעית. אם יש עמו מלאכה
אחרת - כשר; ואם לאו - פסול. אבל אם היה עסוק במלאכתו
כל שני שבוע, כיון שבאת שביעית התחיל מפשט את ידיו ונושא
ונותן בפירות שביעית, אף על פי שאין עמו מלאכה אחרת - כשר.
רבי בא בר זבדא רבי אבהו בשם רבי לעזר: הלכה כרבי יודה

ירושלמי פאה א:א

אי זהו מורא? לא יושב במקומו ולא מדבר במקומו ולא סותר
את דבריו. אי זה הוא כיבוד? מאכיל ומשקה מלביש ומנעיל
מכניס ומוציא. מן דמאן? הונא בר חייא אמר: משל זקן. ואית
דבעי מימר: משלו. לא כן אמר רבי אבהו בשם רבי יוסי בן חנינה:
מניין אפילו אמר לו אביו: השלך את הארנק לים, שישמעלו?
בההוא דאית ליה חורין, ובעושה הנחת רוחו של אביו....
מילתיה דרבי חייא בא ווא אמר: תנא רבי יודן בן דורתי דרבי
שמעון בן יוחי היא. דתני: רבי שמעון בן יוחי אומר: גדול הוא
כיבוד אב ואם שהעדיפו הקדוש ברוך הוא יותר מכיבודו. נאמר:
כבד את אביך ואת אמך, ונאמר: כבד את ה' מהונך; ממה את
מכבדו? משיחננך. מפריש לקט שכחה ופיאה, מפריש תרומה
ומעשר ראשון ומעשר שני ומעשר עני וחלה, ועושה סוכה ולולב
ושופר ותפילין וציצית, ומאכיל את העניים ואת הרעבים, ומשקה
את הצמאים. אם יש לך - את חייב בכל אילו; ואם אין לך -
אין את חייב באחת מהן. אבל כשהוא בא אצל כיבוד אב ואם -
בין שיש לך הון, בין שאין לך הון - כבד את אביך ואת אמך,
ואפילו את מסבב על הפתחים....

אמר רבי בא בר כהנא: השוה הכתוב מצוה קלה שבקלות למצוה
חמורה שבחמורות. מצוה קלה שבקלות - זה שילוח הקן. ומצוה
חמורה שבחמורות - זה כיבוד אב ואם. ובשתיהן כתיב: והארכת
ימים. אמר רבי אבון: ומה אם דבר שהוא פריעת החוב כתיב בו
למען ייטב לך ולמען יאריכו ימיך, דבר שיש בו חסרון כיס וסיכון
נפשות לא כל שכן. אמר רבי לוי: והוא דרבה מנה. גדול הוא דבר
שהוא בפריעת חוב מדבר שאינו בפריעת חוב. תני רבי שמעון בן
יוחי: כשם שמתן שכרן שוה כך פורענותן שוה. מה טעם? עין תלעג
לאב ותבז ליקהת אם - עין שהלעיגה על כיבוד אב ואם וביזת על
לא תקח האם על הבנים. יקרוה עובי נחל - יבוא עורב שהוא

אבון: פטור אני מכיבוד אב ואם. אמרו: כד עברת ליה אימיה
מית אבוי; כד ילדתיה מיתת.

יש שהוא מאכיל את אביו פטומות ויורש גיהנם ויש שהוא כודנו
בריחים ויורש גן עדן. כיצד מאכיל את אביו פטומות ויורש גיהנם?
חד בר נש הוה מייכיל לאבוי תרנגולין פטימין. חד זמן אמר ליה
אבוי: ברי אילין מנן לך? אמר ליה: סבא סבא! אכול ואדיש
דכלביא אכלין ומדשין. נמצא מאכיל את אביו פטומות ויורש
גיהנם. כיצד כודנו בריחים ויורש גן עדן? חד בר נש הוה איטחין
בריחייא אתת צמות לטחונייא. אמר ליה: אבא! עול טחון תחתי;
אין מטת מבזייא טב לי אנא ולא את; אין מטות מילקי טב לי
אנא ולא את. נמצא כודנו בריחים ויורש גן עדן.

נאמר: איש אמו ואביו תיראו, ונאמר: את ה' אלהיך תירא ואתו
תעבד. הקיש מורא אב ואם למורא שמים. נאמר: כבד את אביך
ואת אמך, ונאמר: כבד את ה' מהונך. הקיש כיבוד אב ואם לכבוד
המקום. נאמר: ומקלל אביו ואמו מות יומת, ונאמר: איש איש כי
יקלל אלהיו ונשא חטאו. הקיש קללות אב ואם לקללת המקום.
אבל אי איפשר לומר מכה כלפי למעלן. וכן בדין מפני ששלשתן
שותפין בו.

בבלי נדה לא.

שלשה שותפין יש באדם: הקדוש ברוך הוא ואביו ואמו. אביו
מזריע הלובן שממנו עצמות וגידים וצפרנים ומוח שבראשו ולובן
שבעין. אמו מזרעת אודם שממנו עור ובשר ושהור שבעין.
והקדוש ברוך הוא נותן בו רוח ונשמה וקלסתר פנים וראיית העין
ושמיעת האוזן ודבור פה והולך רגלים ובינה והשכל. וכיון שהגיע
זמנו להפטר מן העולם הקדוש ברוך הוא נוטל חלקו וחלק אביו
ואמו מניח לפניהם.

אצבעתיה דאבוי. ואית דמרין: ריגליה דאבוה הוות פשיטא על
תיבותא. נחת לגבון, אמר לון: לא יכילית מיתותיה לכון. אמרין:
דילמא דו בעי פריטין טובן. אסקוניה למאתים אסקוניה לאלף.
כיון דאיתעיר אבוה מן שינתיה סלק ואייתותיה לון. בעו מיתון
ליה כדפסיקו ליה אחרייא ולא קביל עלוי. אמר: מה אנא מזבין
לכון איקרא דאבהתי בפריטין?! איני נהנה מכבוד אבותי כלום.
מה פרע לו הקדוש ברוך הוא שכר? אמר רבי יוסי בי רבי בון: בו
בלילה ילדה פרתו פרה אדומה ושקלו לו כל ישראל משקלה זהב
ונטלוה. אמר רבי שבתי: כתיב: ומשפט ורב צדקה לא יענה - אין
הקדוש ברוך הוא משהא מתן שכרן של עושי מצות בגוים.
אמו של רבי טרפון ירדה לטייל לתוך חצרה בשבת והלך רבי טרפון
והניח שתי ידיו תחת פרסותיה והיתה מהלכת עליהן עד שהגיעה
למיטתה. פעם אחת חלה ונכנסו חכמים לבקרו. אמרה להן:
התפללו על טרפון בני שהוא נוהג בי כבוד יותר מדאי. אמרו לה:
מהו עבד ליך? ותניית להון עובדא. אמרו לה: אפילו עושה כן אלף
אלפים אדיין לחצי כיבוד שאמרה תורה לא הגיע. אמו של רבי
ישמעאל באה וקבלה עליו לרבותינו. אמרה להן: גערו בישמעאל
בני שאינו נוהג בי בכבוד. באותה שעה נתכרכמו פניהן של רבותינו.
אמרו: איפשר לית רבי ישמעאל נוהג בכבוד אבתיו? אמרו לה:
מה עבד ליך? אמרה: כדו נפק מבית ועדא אנא בעיא משזגה
ריגלוי ומישתי מהן ולא שביק לי. אמרו לו: הואיל והוא רצונה
הוא כבודה. אמר רבי מנא: יאות אילין טחוניא אמרין: כל בר נש
ובר נש זכותיה גו קופתה. אימיה דרבי טרפון אמרה לכון אכין
ואגיבונה אכין; אימיה דרבי ישמעאל אמרה לון אכן ואגיבונה
אכן. רבי זעירא הוה מצטער ואמר: הלואי הוה לי אבא ואימא
דאיקרינהון דנירת גן עדן. כד שמע אילין תרתין אולפניא אמר:
בריך רחמנא דלית לי לא אבא ואימא! לא כרבי טרפון הוה
יכילנא עביד ולא כרבי ישמעאל הוינא מקבלה עלי. אמר רבי

משנה קידושין א:ב

עבד עברי נקנה בכסף ובשטר. וקונה את עצמו בשנים וביובל
ובגרעון כסף. יתרה עליו אמה העבריה שקונה את עצמה בסימנין.
הנרצע נקנה ברציעה. וקונה את עצמו ביובל ובמיתת האדון.

ירושלמי קידושין א:ב

תני: רבי אליעזר בן יעקב אומר: ולמה אל הדלת? שעל ידי דלת
יצאו מעבדות לחירות. שאלו התלמידים את רבן יוחנן בן זכאי:
מה ראה העבד הזה לירצע באזנו יותר מכל איבריו? אמר להן:
אוזן ששמעה מהר סיני: לא יהיה לך אלהים אחרים על פני,
ופירקה מעליה עול מלכות שמים וקיבלה עליה עול בשר ודם; אוזן
ששמעה לפני הר סיני: כי לי בני ישראל עבדים, והלך זה וקנה אדון
אחר; לפיכך תבוא האוזן ותירצע לפי שלא שמר מה ששמעה אזנו.

משנה פאה א:א

אלו דברים שאין להם שיעור: הפאה והבכורים והראיון וגמילות
חסדים ותלמוד תורה. אלו דברים שאדם אוכל פרותיהן בעולם
הזה והקרן קימת לו לעולם הבא: כבוד אב ואם וגמילות חסדים
והבאת שלום בין אדם לחברו; ותלמוד תורה כנגד כלם.

ירושלמי פאה א:א

רבי אבהו בשם רבי יוחנן: שאלו את רבי אליעזר: עד היכן הוא
כיבוד אב ואם? אמר להן: ולי אתם שואלין? לכו ושאלו את דמה
בן נתינה. דמה בן נתינה ראש פטרבולי היה פעם אחת היתה אמו
מסטרתו בפני כל בולי שלו ונפל קורדקון שלה מידה והושיט לה
שלא תצטער. אמר רבי חזקיה: גוי אשקלוני היה וראש פטרבולי
היה ואבן שישב עליה אביו לא ישב עליה מימיו וכיון שמת אביו
עשה אותה יראה שלו. פעם אחת אבדה ישפה של בנימן. אמרו:
מאן דאית ליה טבא דכוותה? אמרו: אית לדמה בן נתינה. אזלון
לגביה ופסקו עימיה במאה דינר. סליק בעי מייתה להו ואשכח
אבוה דמיך. ואית דאמרין: מפתחא דתיבותא הוה יתיב גו

ותחילה לארבעים. אמר להן משה: ארבעין יומין אנא מיעבד
בטורא. כיון שהגיע יום ארבעים ולא בא מיד: וירא העם כי בשש
משה לרדת מן ההר. וכיון שהגיע שש שעות ולא בא מיד: ויקהל
העם על אהרן ויאמרו אליו קום עשה לנו אלהים אשר ילכו לפנינו
וגו'. וידבר ה' אל משה לך רד כי שחת עמך וגו'. וישמע יהושע את
קול העם ברעה ויאמר אל משה קול מלחמה במחנה. אמר משה:
אדם שהוא עתיד להנהיג שררה על ששים ריבוא אינו יודע להבחין
בין קול לקול! ויאמר אין קול ענות גבורה ואין קול ענות חלושה
קול ענות אנכי שומע. אמר רבי יסא: קול קילוס עבודת כוכבים
אנכי שומע....

ויחר אף משה וישלך מידיו את הלחת וישבר אתם תחת ההר. תני
רבי ישמעאל: הקדוש ברוך הוא אמר לו שישברם, שנאמר: ואכתב
על הלחת את הדברים אשר היו על הלחת הראשונים אשר שברת.
אמר לו: יפה עשית ששיברת. רבי שמואל בר נחמן בשם רבי
יונתן: הלחות היו אורכן ששה טפחים ורחבן שלשה, והיה משה
תפיש בטפחיים והקדוש ברוך הוא בטפחיים וטפחיים ריוח
באמצע. כיון שעשו ישראל אותו מעשה ביקש הקדוש ברוך הוא
לחוטפן מידו של משה. וגברה ידו של משה וחטפן ממנו; הוא
שהכתוב משבחו בסוף ואומר: ולכל היד החזקה - ייא שלמא על
ידה דגברת עליה מינאי. רבי יוחנן בשם רבי יוסה בר אביי אמר
ליה: הלוחות היו מבקשין לפרוח והיה משה תופשין, דכתיב:
ואתפש בשני הלחת. תני בשם רבי נחמיה: הכתב עצמו פרח. רבי
עזרה בשם רבי יהודה בי רבי סימון: הלוחות היו משאוי ארבעים
סאה והכתב היה סובלן. כיון שפרח הכתב כבדו על ידיו של משה
ונפלו ונשתברו....

תני רבי שמעון בן יוחי: רבי עקיבא רבי היה דורש: כה אמר ה'
צבאות צום הרביעי וצום החמישי וצום השביעי וצום העשירי וגו'.
צום הרביעי - זה י"ט בתמוז, שנשתברו הלוחות ובטל התמיד
והובקעה העיר ושרף אפוסטומוס את התורה והעמיד צלם בהיכל.

דמלתא אמרה: צריך בר נש חשש על לווטייא דרבה, אפילו על
מגן. רבי ירמיה בשם רבי שמואל בר יצחק: מגילה שמסר שמואל
לדוד אמרה אחיתופל ברוח הקודש. ומה הוה אחיתופל עביד? כד
הוה בר נש אזל ממלך ביה במילה, הוה אמר ליה: איזיל עביד כן
והכן; ואין לית את מהימן לי, אזל ושאיל באורים ותומים. והוה
אזל שאל ומשכח ליה כן; הדא היא דכתיב: ועצת אחיתופל אשר
יעץ בימים ההם כאשר ישאל וגוי....
כיצד נתרחק? ואחיתופל ראה כי לא נעשתה עצתו ויחבוש את
חמורו וגוי. שלשה דברים צוה אחיתופל את בניו; אמר להם: אל
תמרדו במלכות בית דוד, דאשכחן דקודשא בריך הוא נסיב לון
אפין אפילו בפרהסיא; ואל תשאו ותתנו עם מי שהשעה משחקת
לון; ואם היתה העצרת ברורה זרעו חטים יפות. ולא ידעין אם
ברורה בטל ואם ברורה בשרב.

משנה אבות ה:ו
עשרה דברים נבראו בערב שבת בין השמשות, ואלו הן: פי הארץ,
ופי הבאר, ופי האתון, והקשת, והמן, והמטה, והשמיר, והכתב,
והמכתב, והלוחות....

משנה תענית ד:ה
חמשה דברים ארעו את אבותינו בשבעה עשר בתמוז וחמשה
בתשעה באב. בשבעה עשר בתמוז נשתברו הלוחות ובטל התמיד
והבקעה העיר ושרף אפסטמוס את התורה והעמיד צלם בהיכל.
בתשעה באב נגזר על אבותינו שלא יכנסו לארץ וחרב הבית
בראשונה ובשניה ונלכדה בתר ונחרשה העיר. משנכנס אב ממעטין
בשמחה.
ירושלמי תענית ד:ה
כתיב: וישכן כבוד ה' על הר סיני ויכסהו הענן ששת ימים ויקרא
אל משה ביום השביעי ויעל משה - שביעי שהוא לאחר הדיברות,

אחיתופל אדם גיבור בתורה היה. כתיב: ויוסף עוד דוד את כל
בחור בישראל שלשים אלף. רבי ברכיה בשם רבי אבא בר כהנא:
תשעים אלף זקינים מינה דוד ביום אחד, ולא מינה אחיתופל
עמהן; הדא היא דכתיב: ויוסף עוד דוד את כל בחור בישראל
שלשים אלף. ויוסף - תלתין; עוד - תלתין; ופשוטיה דקרייא -
תלתין: הרי תשעין. את מוצא בשעה שבא דוד לשאת את ארון
ברית ה' לא נשאו כתורה: וירכיבו את ארון ברית האלוהים על
עגלה חדשה וגו'. והוה ארונא טעון כהניא לרומא וטרוף לון
לארעא, טעון כהניא לרומא וטריף לון לארעא. שלח דוד ואייתי
לאחיתופל. אמר ליה: לית את אמר לי מה לדין ארונא, דו טעון
כהניא לרומא טריף לון לארעא, טעון כהניא לרומא וטריף לון
לארעא? אמר ליה: שלח שאול לאילין חכימייא דמניתא! אמר
דוד: מאן דידע למיקמתה ולא מקימה - יהא סיפיה מתחנקה!
אמר: דבח קומי והוא קאים, הדא היא דכתיב: ויהי כי צעדו
נושאי ארון ה' ששה צעדים ויזבחו שור ומריא....
אמר הקדוש ברוך הוא לאחיתופל: מילה דמיינקייא אמרין
בכנישתא בכל יום לא אמרת ליה! ולבני קהת לא נתן כי עבודת
הקודש עליהם בכתף ישאו; ודא אמרת ליה?! וכן את מוצא
בשעה שבא דוד לחפור תימליוסים של בית המקדש, חפר חמש
עשר מאוין דאמין ולא אשכח תהומא. ובסופא אשכח חד עציץ
ובעה מירמיתיה. אמר ליה: לית את יכיל! אמר ליה: למה? אמר
ליה: דנא הכה כביש על תהומא. אמר ליה: ומן אימת את הכא?
אמר ליה: מן שעתא דאשמע רחמנא קליה בסיני: אנכי ה' אלהיך;
רעדת ארעא ושקיעת ואנא יהיב הכא כביש על תהומא. אף על גב
כן לא שמע ליה. כיון דרימיה, סליק תהומא ובעה מטפא עלמא.
והוה אחיתופל קאים תמן, אמר: כדין דוד מתחנק ואנא מליך.
אמר דוד: מאן דחכם דידע מקימתיה ולא מקים ליה - ייא סופיה
מתחנק! אמר מה דאמר, ואוקמיה....
אף על גב כן הוה סופה מתחנקה. אמר רבי יוסי: הדא היא

כתיפיו. הנס הששי - כיון שיצא וראה את הנגף שהוא מחבל
בעם, מה עשה? השליכן לארץ ועמד ונתפלל; הדא הוא דכתיב:
ויעמד פינחס ויפלל ותעצר המגפה.

כשבאו ישראל לנקום נקמת מדין מצאו שם בלעם בן בעור. וכי
מה בא לעשות? בא ליטול שכר עשרים וארבעה אלף שמתו
מישראל על ידו בשיטים. אמר ליה פינחס: לא דברייך עבדת ולא
דבלק עבדת. לא דברייך עבדת - דמר לך: לא תיזול עם שלוחי
בלק, ואזלת. ולא דבלק עבדת - דאמר לך: איזיל לייט ישראל,
וברכתנון. אף אני איני מקפחך שכרך; הדא הוא דכתיב: ואת
בלעם בן בעור הקוסם הרגו בני ישראל על חלליהם. מהו: על
חלליהם? שהיה שקול כנגד כל חלליהם. דבר אחר: על חלליהם -
מה חלליהם אין בהן ממש אף הוא אין בו ממש. דבר אחר: על
חלליהם - שהיה צף כנגד כל חלליהם והיה פינחס מראה לו את
הציץ והוא שוקע ויורד. דבר אחר: על חלליהם - אלא מלמד
שנתנו לו ישראל שכרו משלם ולא קיפחוהו.

דואג אדם גדול בתורה היה. באו ישראל ושאלו את דוד: לחם
הפנים מהו שידחה את השבת? אמר להם: סידורו דוחה את
השבת; לא לישתו ולא עריכתו דוחין את השבת. והיה שם דואג,
ואמר: מי הוא זה שבא להורות לפניי? אמרו לו: דוד בן ישי הוא.
מיד הלך ונתן עצה לשאול מלך ישראל להמית את נוב עיר
הכהנים; הדא היא דכתיב: ויאמר המלך לרצים הניצבים עליו
סובו והמיתו את כהני ה' כי גם ידם עם דוד וגו'....

ויאמר המלך לדוייג ... סוב אתה ופגע בכהני ה'. ויסב דואג
האדומי ויפגע בכהנים וגו'. לא כן תני רבי חייא: אין ממנין שני
כהנים גדולים כאחת? אלא מלמד שהיו כולם ראויין להיות כהנים
גדולים. כיצד נתרחק? רבי חנינה ורבי יהושע בן לוי - חד אמר:
אש יצאה מבית קדשי הקדשים וליהטה סביבותיו; וחרנה אמר:
תלמידים ותיקים נזדווגו לו והיו למידים והוא שכח, לקיים מה
שנאמר: חיל בלע ויקיאנו מבטנו יורישנו אל.

ירושלמי סנהדרין יא:ו

אמר רבי יוסי בן חנינה: הכל היה בכלל: לא תענה ברעך עד שקר;
יצא לידון בין באות בין במופת בין בעבודה זרה בין בשאר כל
המצות....

שני נביאים שנתנבאו כאחת, שני נביאים שנתנבאו בכרך אחד: רבי
יצחק ורבי הושעיה - חד אמר: צריך ליתן אות ומופת; וחרנא
אמר: אינו צריך ליתן אות ומופת. מתיב מאן דאמר צריך למאן
דאמר אינו צריך, והא כתיב: ויאמר חזקיהו אל ישעיהו מה אות.
אמר ליה: שנייא היא תמן דו עסק בתחיית המתים: יחיינו מיומים
ביום השלישי יקימנו ונחיה לפניו.

ירושלמי סנהדרין י:ב

והנה איש מבני ישראל בא ויקרב אל אחיו את המדיינית לעיני
משה. מהו לעיני משה? כאינש דמר: הא גו עינך משה! אמר לון:
אין צפורך מדינית ואין טלפיה סדוקות? זו טהורה וזו טמאה?!
והיה שם פינחס, אמר: אין כאן אדם שיהרגנו ויהרג על ידיו?...
כיון שראה פינחס שאין אדם מישראל עושה כלום מיד עמד פינחס
מתוך סנהדרין שלו ולקח את הרומח בידו ונתן את הברזל תחת
פסיקייא שלו. התחיל מסתמך על עץ שלה עד שהגיע לפתחו. כיון
שהגיע לפיתחו, אמר לו: מאיין ולאיין פינחס? אמר להן: אין אתם
מודים לי ששבטו של לוי אצל שבטו של שמעון בכל מקום? אמרו:
הניחו לו שמא התירו פרושים את הדבר. כיון שנכנס עשה לו
הקדוש ברוך הוא ששה ניסים: הנס הראשון - דרכן לפרוש זה
מזה, והדביקן המלאך זה לזה. הנס השני - כיון את הרומח כנגד
הקיבה שלה כדי שתהא זכרותו נראית מתוך קיבה שלה, מפני
הנוקרנין שלא יהו אומרין: אף הוא בין כתיפיו נכנס עמהן ועשה
את צרכיו. הנס השלישי - סתם המלאך את פיהן ולא היו יכולין
לצווח. הנס הרביעי - לא נשמטו מן הזיין אלא עמדו במקומן.
הנס החמישי - הגביה לו המלאך את השקוף כדי שיצאו שניהן בין

היכנס ובור לך! וכיון שהיה נכנס היה שם צרצור מלא יין מן היין
העמוני, שהוא קשה והוא את הגוף מפתה לזנות והיה ריחו מפעפע
- ועדיין לא נאסר יינן יין נסך של נכרים על ישראל - והיתה
אומרת לו: רצונך לשתות כוס יין? והוא אומר לה: הין! והיא
נותנת לו והוא שותה. וכיון שהיה שותה היה היין בוער בו ככריסה
של חכינה. והוא אומר לה: הישמעו לי. והיא אומרת לו: רצונך
שאשמע לך? והוא אומר: הין! מיד היתה מוציאה לו טפוס של
פעור מתוך חיקה שלה, והיתה אומרת לו: השתחוה לזה ואני
נשמעת לך. והוא אומר לה: וכי לעבודה זרה אני משתחוה?! והיתה
אומרת לו: אין את משתחוה אלא במגלה עצמך לו. זו היא
שאמרו חכמים: הפוער עצמו לבעל פעור - זו היא עבודתו; והזורק
אבן למרקוליס - זו היא עבודתו....

והיתה אומרת לו: הינזר מתורת משה ואני נשמעת לך. הדא הוא
דכתיב: המה באו בעל פעור וינזרו לבושת ויהיו שיקוצים כאהבם
- עד שנעשו שיקוצים לאביהם שבשמים. אמר רבי לעזר: מה
המסמר הזה אי אפשר לו לפרוש מן הדלת בלא עץ, כך אי אפשר
לפרוש מן הפעור בלא נפשות. מעשה בסובתה מאולם, שהשכיר
חמורו לגויה אחת להשתחוות לפעור. כיון שהגיעו לביתו של פעור,
אמרה לו: המתן לו כאן עד שאיכנס ואשתחוה לפעור. כיון שיצאת,
אמר לה: המתיני לי כאן עד שאיכנס ואעשה כמות שעשית. מה
עשה? נכנס ועשה את צרכיו וקינח עצמו בחוטמו של פעור. והיו
הכל מקלסין לפניו ואומרים: לא עשה אדם כשם שעשה זה!

משנה סנהדרין יא:ו

המתנבא בשם עבודה זרה ואומר: כך אמרה עבודה זרה - אפילו
כוון את ההלכה לטמא את הטמא ולטהר את הטהור. הבא על
אשת איש - כיון שנכנסה לרשות הבעל לנשואין אף על פי שלא
נבעלה הבא עליה הרי זה בחנק. וזוממי בת כהן ובועלה שכל
הזוממין מקדימין לאותה המיתה חוץ מזוממי בת כהן ובועלה.

לאחיו - לא שישלם ממון? וכא הכל היה בכלל: וכל זר לא יאכל
קודש; יצא: ואיש כי יאכל קודש בשגגה - שישלם ממון! והתני:
מודין חכמים לרבי מאיר בגונב תרומת חבירו ואכלו שהוא לוקה
ומשלם.... שכן האוכל חלבו לוקה.

משנה פאה א:א

אלו דברים שאדם אוכל פרותיהן בעולם הזה והקרן קיימת לו
לעולם הבא: כיבוד אב ואם וגמילות חסדים והבאת שלום בין
אדם לחברו; ותלמוד תורה כנגד כלם.

משנה סנהדרין י:ב

שלשה מלכים וארבעה הדיוטות אין להם חלק לעולם הבא. שלשה
מלכים: ירבעם אחאב ומנשה. רבי יהודה אומר: מנשה יש לו חלק
לעולם הבא, שנאמר: ויתפלל אליו ויעתר לו וישמע תחינתו
וישיבהו ירושלם למלכותו. אמרו לו: למלכותו השיבו ולא לחיי
העולם הבא השיבו. ארבעה הדיוטות: בלעם ודואג ואחיתפל
וגחזי.

ירושלמי סנהדרין י:ב

וכי מה עשה בלעם הרשע? על ידי שנתן עצה לבלק בן צפור להפיל
את ישראל בחרב. אמר לו: אלוה של אומה הזו הוא שונה את
זנות; אלא העמידו בנותיכם בזימה ואתם שולטין בהן. אמר ליה:
ומישמע לי אינון? אמר ליה: אקים בנתך קומי וינון חמיין ושמעין
לך. הדא דכתיב: ראש אומות בית אב במדין הוא. מה עשו? בנו
להן קנקלין מבית הישימון עד הר השלג והושיבו שם נשים מוכרת
מיני כיסניון. הושיבו את הזקינה מבחוץ ואת הנערה מבפנים. והיו
ישראל אוכלין ושותין והיה מהן אחד יוצא לטייל בשוק ולוקח לו
חפץ מן החנווני והיתה הזקינה מוכרת לו את החפץ בשיוויו. והנערא
אומרת לו: בא וטול לך בפחות. כן ביום הראשון וכן ביום השני
וכן ביום השלישי. והיתה אומרת לו: מיכן והילך אתה כבן בית

בין שכלל ואחר כך פרט, בין שפרט ואחר כך כלל; כלל ופרט הוא
בשבת - כלל בעבודתה ופרט בעבודתה. ובעבודה זרה - כלל
בעבודתה ופרט למלאכת הגבוה.

משנה כתובות ג:א

אלו נערות שיש להן קנס: הבא על הממזרת ועל הנתינה ועל
הכותית; הבא על הגיורת ועל השבויה ועל השפחה שנפדו ושנתגיירו
ושנשתחררו פחותות מבנות שלש שנים ויום אחד; הבא על אחותו
ועל אחות אביו ועל אחות אמו ועל אחות אשתו ועל אשת אחיו
ועל אשת אחי אביו ועל הנדה - יש להן קנס. אף על פי שהן
בהכרת אין בהן מיתת בית דין.

ירושלמי כתובות ג:א

נתן בר הושעיה אמר: כאן בנערה וכאן בבוגרת: נערה יש לה קנס
ואין לה מכות; בוגרת יש לה מכות ואין לה קנס. ואין לה בושת
ופגס? רבנין דקסרין אמרין: תיפתר שהפיתתו או שמחלה לו.
וסבר נתן בר הושעיה: במקום מכות ותשלומין, משלם ואינו לוקה
וילקה וישלם? כדי רשעתו - משום רשעה אחת אתה מחייבו ואי
אתה מחייבו משום שתי רשעיות. וישלם ולא ילקה כעדים זוממין
כמה דתימר תמן בעדים זוממין: משלמין ואין לוקין, וכא: משלם
ואינו לוקה. אמר רבי יונה: טעמא דרבי נתן בר הושעיה: כדי
רשעתו - את שמכותיו יוצאות; כדי רשעתו - יצא זה שאומרים
לו: עמוד ושלם. מתניתא פליגא על רבי שמעון בן לקיש: האוכל
תרומה מזיד משלם את הקרן ואינו משלם את החומש. על
דעתיה דנתן בר הושעיה, דאמר: משלם - ניחא. על דעתיה דרבי
יוחנן, דאמר: התרו בו, לוקה; ואם לא התרו בו, משלם - פתר לה
מזיד בלא בהתראה. על דעתיה דרבי שמעון בן לקיש לא שנייא
היא שוגג היא מזיד היא התרו בו היא לא התרו בו....
רבי שמעון בן לקיש כדעתיה, כמה דו אמר תמן: הכל היה בכלל:
לא תענה ברעך עד שקר: יצא: ועשיתם לו כאשר זמם לעשות

מסייא לריש לקיש: תורה אחת יהיה לכם לעושה בשגגה. אין לי
אלא דבר שהוא מעשה; המגדף והמשתחוה שאינן מעשה מניין?

ברייתא דרבי ישמעאל פרשה א:א

רבי ישמעאל אומר: בשלש עשרי מדות התורה נדרשת....
מכלל ופרט - כיצד? מן הבהמה, כלל. מן הבקר ומן הצאן, פרט.
כלל ופרט אין בכלל אלא מה שבפרט.

ירושלמי נזיר ו:א

תני רב זכיי קומי רבי יוחנן: זיבח וקיטר וניסך הבעלם אחד חייב
על כל אחת ואחת. אמר ליה רבי יוחנן: בבלייא! עברת בידך
תלתא נהרין ואתבדת ואינו חייב אלא אחת. עד דלא יתברינה
בידיה יש כאן אחת ואין כאן הנה; מן דתברה בידיה יש כאן הנה
ואין כאן אחת. רבי בא בר ממל בעה קומי רבי זעירא: ויהא חייב
על כל אחת, כמה דתימא בשבת: לא תעשה כל מלאכה - כלל;
לא תבערו אש בכל מושבותיכם - פרט. והלא הבערה בכלל היה?
ויצא מן הכלל ללמד מה הבערה מיוחדת מעשה יחידים וחייבין
עליה בפני עצמה, אף כל מעשה ומעשה שיש בו לחייב עליו בפני
עצמו. וכא: לא תעבדם - כלל; לא תשתחוה - פרט. והלא
השתחויה בכלל היה? ולמה יצאת מן הכלל? ללמד לומר לך: מה
השתחויה מיוחדת מעשה יחידים והייבין עליה בפני עצמה, אף כל
מעשה ומעשה שיש בה לחייב עליו בפני עצמו. אמר לך: בשבת,
כלל במקום אחד ופרט במקום אחר; ובעבודה זרה, כלל שהוא
בצד הערט. אמר ליה: והכתיב: לא תשתחוה לאל אחר; הרי שכלל
במקום אחד ופרט במקום אחר. אמר ליה: מכיון שאין את למד
מצידו אפילו ממקום אחר אי את למד. חברייא אמרי: לא שנייא
היא בין שכלל במקום אחד ופרט במקום אחר, בין שכלל ופרט
במקום אחד; כלל ופרט הוא בשבת - כלל ואחר כך פרט.
ובעבודה זרה - פרט ואחר כך כלל. רבי יוסי אומר: לא שנייא

ירושלמי סנהדרין ז:ט

אזהרה לעובד עבודה זרה מניין? לא תעבדם. כרת מניין? את ה׳
הוא מגדף ונכרתה. ולא מגדף כתיב כאדם שהוא אומר לחבירו:
גירפתה את כל הקערה ולא שיירתה בה כלום. משל רבי שמעון בן
לעזר אומר: לשנים שהיו יושבין וקערה של גריסין ביניהון; פשט
אחד את ידו וגירף את כל הקערה ולא שייר בה כלום. כך המגדף
והעובד עבודה זרה אינו משייר לאחריו מצוה. עונש מניין? והוצאת
האיש ההוא או את האשה ההיא אשר עשו את הדבר הזה אל
שעריך וגו׳, עד: וסקלתם אותם באבנים ומתו. לא תעבדם -
הייתי אומר: עד שיעבוד כל עבודה זרה שבעולם; תלמוד לומר: לא
תשתחוה להם. השתחויה בכלל היתה ולמה יצאת להקיש אליה?
אלא מה השתחויה מיוחדת מעשה יחיד וחייבין עליה בפני עצמה,
אף אני מרבה כל מעשה ומעשה שיש בה חייבין עליו בפני עצמו.
אף על גב דרבי שמעון בן אלעזר אמר: זיבח וקיטר וניסך בהעלם
אחד אינו חייב אלא אחת, מודה שאם עבדה בעבודתה, בעבודת
הגבוה, בעבודת השתחויה, שהוא חייב על כל אחת ואחת....
מניין לאומר לו: אלי אתה? רב אבון בשם רבנין דתמן: וישתחוו לו
ויזבחו לו ויאמרו אלה אלהיך ישראל וגו׳. מעתה אינו מתחייב עד
שיזבח ויקטר ויאמר. אמר רבי יוסי: לא בא הכתוב להזכיר אלא
גניין של ישראל. וישתחוו לו - לא לגבוה; ויזבחו לו - לא לגבוה;
ויאמרו לו - לא לגבוה. מאי כדון? נאמר כאן: אמירה, ונאמר:
אמירה, במסית. מה אמירה האמורה במסית עשה בה אמירה
כמעשה, אף אמירה האמורה כאן נעשה בה אמירה כמעשה....
רבי שמואל בר נחמני בשם רבי הושעיה: האומר לו: אלי אתה -
מחלוקת רבי וחכמים. השתחוה לה מהו? רבי יוחנן אמר: דברי
הכל מודים בכפיפת קומה שהוא חייב. מה בין המעלה והמוריד
קומתו, ומה בין המעלה והמוריד שפתותיו? רבי יוחנן אמר:
במחלוקת; ריש לקיש אמר: במחלוקת. אמר רבי זעירא: קרייא

שנאמר: האשה המנאפת תחת אשה תקח את זרים; וכתוב:

ויאמר ה' אלי עוד לך אהב אשת אהובה רע ומנאפת וגו'.

כתיב: לא תשא את שם ה' אלהיך לשוא, וכנגדו כתיב: לא תגנוב

- מגיד הכתוב שכל מי שהוא גונב בא לסוף לידי שבועת שוא,

שנאמר: הגנוב רצוח ונאוף והשבע לשקר; וכתיב: אלה וכחש ורצוח

וגנוב ונאוף.

כתיב: זכור את יום השבת לקדשו וכנגדו כתיב: לא תענה - מגיד

הכתוב שכל מי שמחלל את השבת מעיד לפני מי שאמר והיה

העולם שלא ברא עולמו לששה ימים ולא נח בשביעי. וכל מי

שמשמר את השבת מעיד לפני מי שאמר והיה העולם שברא

עולמו לששה ימים ונח בשביעי, שנאמר: ואתם עדי נאום ה' ואני

אל.

כתיב: כבד את אביך ואת אמך, וכנגדו כתיב: לא תחמוד - מגיד

הכתוב שכל מי שהוא חומד סוף מוליד בן שהוא מקלל את אביו

ואת אמו ומכבד למי שאינו אביו.

לכך נתנו עשרת הדברות חמשה על לוח זה וחמשה על לוח זה,

דברי רבי חנינא בן גמליאל. וחכמים אומרים: עשרה על לוח זה

ועשרה על לוח זה, שנאמר: את הדברים האלה דבר ה' - ויכתבם

על שני לוהות אבנים; ואומר: שני שדיך כשני עפרים תאומי צביה;

ואומר: ידיו גלילי זהב ממולאים בתרשיש.

משנה סנהדרין ז:ו

העובד עבודה זרה - אחד העובד ואחד הזובח ואחד המקטר ואחד

המנסך ואחד המשתחוה ואחד המקבלו עליו לאלוה והאומר לו

אלי אתה. אבל המגפף והמנשק והמכבד והמרבץ והמרחיץ הסך

המלביש והמנעיל - עובר בלא תעשה. הנודר בשמו והמקים

בשמו - עובר בלא תעשה. הפוער עצמו לבעל פעור - זו היא

עבודתו. הזורק אבן למרקוליס - זו היא עבודתו.

לא תחמוד. רבי אומר: כתוב אחד אומר לא יחמוד וכתוב אחד
אומר לא תתאוה. כיצד יתקיימו שני מקראות הללו? הרי זה
אזהרה לעוקף אחר הנואף. לא תחמוד בית רעך - כלל; ועבדו
ואמתו ושורו וחמורו - פרט. כלל ופרט אין בכלל אלא מה
שבפרט. וכשהוא אומר: וכל אשר לרעך, חזר וכלל; אי כל ככלל
הראשון הרי אמרת לאו. אלא חזר וכלל - כלל ופרט וכלל אי אתה
דן אלא כעין הפרט: מה הפרט מפורש בדבר שהוא קונה ומקנה
אף כל בדבר שהוא קונה ומקנה. אי מה הפרט מפורש בנכסים
המטלטלין שאין להם אחריות אף אין לי אלא נכסים המטלטלין
שאין להם אחריות. וכשהוא אומר במשנה תורה: שדהו, על כרחך
מה הפרט מפורש בדבר שהוא קונה ומקנה אף אין לי אלא בדבר
שהוא קונה ומקנה. אי מה הפרט מפורש בדבר שאינו בא
ברשותך אלא ברצון בעלים, אף אין לי אלא דבר שאי אפשר לבא
ברשותך אלא ברצון בעלים. יצא שאתה חומד בתו לבנך או בנו
לבתך. או אפילו חומד בדיבור? תלמוד לומר: לא תחמוד כסף
וזהב עליהם ולקחת לך, מה להלן עד שעושה מעשה, אף כאן עד
שעושה מעשה.

מכילתא בחדש ח

כיצד נתנו עשרת הדברות? חמשה על לוח זה וחמשה על לוח זה.
כתיב: אנכי ה' אלהיך, וכנגדו: לא תרצח - מגיד הכתוב שכל מי
ששופך דם מעלה עליו הכתוב כאלו ממעט בדמות המלך. משל
למלך בשר ודם שנכנס למדינה והעמיד לו איקונות ועשה לו צלמים
וטבעו לו מטבעות. לאחר זמן כפו לו איקונותיו שברו לו צלמיו
ובטלו לו מטבעותיו ומיעטו בדמות של מלך. כך כל מי שהוא
שופך דמים מעלה עליו הכתוב כאלו ממעט בדמות המלך, שנאמר:
שופך דם האדם וגו' כי בצלם אלהים עשה את האדם.
כתיב: לא יהיה לך, וכתיב כנגדו: לא תנאף - מגיד הכתוב שכל מי
שעובד עבודה זרה מעלה עליו הכתוב כאלו מנאף אחר המקום,

ואומר: ועד זקנה אני הוא. ואומר: כה אמר ה' מלך ישראל וגואלו
ה' צבאות אני ראשון ואני אחרון. ואומר: מי פעל ועשה קורא
הדורות מראש אני ה' ראשון ואת אחרונים אני הוא. רבי נתן
אומר: מכאן תשובה למינין שאומרים שתי רשויות הן. שכשעמד
הקדוש ברוך הוא ואמר אנכי ה' אלהיך מי עמד ומיחה כנגדו? אם
תאמר במטמניות היה הדבר והלא כבר נאמר: לא בסתר דברתי
וגו' לאלו אני נותנה אלא לא אמרתי - להם - תוהו בקשוני ולא
נתתיה פגגס. וכן הוא אומר: אני ה' דובר צדק מגיד מישרים.

מכילתא בחדש ח

לא תרצח. למה נאמר? לפי שנאמר: שופך דם האדם, עונש שמענו;
אזהרה לא שמענו. תלמוד לומר: לא תרצח.

לא תנאף. למה נאמר? לפי שהוא אומר: מות יומת הנואף
והנואפת, עונש שמענו; אזהרה לא שמענו. תלמוד לומר: לא תנאף.

לא תגנוב. למה נאמר? לפי שהוא אומר: וגונב איש ומכרו, עונש
שמענו; אזהרה מנין? תלמוד לומר: לא תגנוב. הרי זה אזהרה
לגונב נפש; אתה אומר לגונב נפש או אינו אלא אזהרה לגונב
ממון? כשהוא אומר: לא תגנובו, הרי אזהרה לגונב ממון. הא מה
תלמוד לומר: לא תגנוב? בגונג נפשות הכתוב מדבר. או הרי זה
לגונב ממון, והלא אזהרה לגונב נפש. אמרת: צא ולמד משלש
עשרה מדות. ועוד אמרת: שלש מצות נאמרו בענין זה שתים
מפורשות ואחת סתומה. נלמד סתומה ממפורשות: מה מפורשות
מצות שחייבין עליהן מיתת בית דין אף סתומה מצוה שחייבין
עליה מיתת בית דין. הא אין עליך לומר כלשון אחרון אלא כלשון
ראשון: הרי זה אזהרה לגונב נפש והלה אזהרה לגונב ממון.

לא תענה ברעך וגו'. למה נאמר? לפי שהוא אומר: ועשיתם לו
כאשר זמם לעשות לאחיו, עונש שמענו; אזהרה לא שמענו. תלמוד
לומר: לא תענה ברעך וגו'.

ירושלמי בבא קמא ד:ו

ואיש כי יכה כל נפש אדם: להביא את המכה ויש בו כדי להמית. אית תניי תני: אין בו כדי להמית. אמר רבי לא: ואפילו יש בו כדי להמית ובא אחר והמית - הממית חייב.

מכילתא בחדש ה

אנכי ה' אלהיך. מפני מה לא נאמרו עשרת הדברות בתחילת התורה? משלו משל למה הדבר דומה: לאחד שנכנס במדינה, אמר להם: אמלוך עליכם. אמרו לו: כלום עשית לנו טובה שתמלוך עלינו. מה עשה? בנה להם את החומה הכניס להם את המים עשה להם מלחמות. אמר להם: אמלוך עליכם. אמרו לו: הן והן. כך המקום הוציא את ישראל ממצרים קרע להם את הים הוריד להם את המן העלה להם את הבאר הגיז להם את השלו עשה להם מלחמת עמלק. אמר להם: אמלוך עליהם. אמרו לו: הן והן. רבי אומר: להודיע שבחן של ישראל שכשעמדו כולן על הר סיני לקבל התורה השוו כולם לב אחד לקבל מלכות שמים בשמחה. ולא עוד אלא שהיו ממשכנין עצמן זה על זה. ולא על הנגלות בלבד נגלה הקדוש ברוך הוא עליהם לכרות ברית עמהם אלא אף על הסתרים. אמרו לו: על הגלויים אנו כורתים ברית עמך ולא על הסתרים שלא יהא יהא ממנו אחד חוטא בסתר ויהא הצבור מתמשכן, שנאמר: הנסתרות לה' אלהינו והנגלות לנו ולבנינו.

אנכי ה' אלהיך. למה נאמר? לפי שנגלה על הים כגבור עושה מלחמות, שנאמר: ה' איש מלחמה. נגלה על הר סיני כזקן מלא רחמים, שנאמר: ויראו את אלהי ישראל. וכשנגאלו מה הוא אומר? וכעצם השמים לטוהר. ואומר: הזה הוית עד די כרסון רמיו. ואומר: נהר דינור נגד ונפק מן קדמוהי וגו'. שלא ליתן פתחון פה לאומות העולם לומר שתי רשויות הן. אלא אני ה' אלהיך - אני במצרים אני על הים אני בסיני אני לשעבר אני לעתיד לבא אני לעולם הזה אני לעולם הבא, שנאמר: ראו עתה כי אני אני הוא.

משנה בבא קמא ה:ז

אחד השור ואחד כל הבהמות לנפילת הבור ולהפרשת הר סיני ולתשלומי כפל ולהשבת אבדה לפריקה לחסימה לכלאים ולשבת, וכן חיה ואוף כיוצא בהן. אם כן למה נאמר שור או חמור? אלא שדבר הכתוב בהווה.

ירושלמי בבא קמא ה:ח

לשבת? למען ינוח שורך וחמורך.

משנה גיטין ח:ג

היתה עומדת על ראש הגג וזרקו לה - כיון שהגיע לאויר הגג הרי זו מגרשת. הוא מלמעלה והיא מלמטה וזרקו לה - כיון שיצא מרשות הגג נמחק או נשרף הרי זו מגרשת.

ירושלמי גיטין ח:ג

אמר רבי אלעזר: מתניתא בגג שיש לו מעקה והוא שירד לאויר מעקה. ושאין לו מעקה והוא שירד לאויר שלשה שהן סמוכין לגג, שכל שלשה שהן סמוכין לגג כגג הן. רבי יעקב בר אחא רבי בא בר המנונא בשם רב אדא בר אחווה: לענין שבת, שכל שלשה שהן סמוכין למחיצה כמחיצה הן. אמר רבי יסא: דלא דמיא, גיטין מלמעלן ושבת מלמטן; גיטין אפילו לא נח שבת עד שינוח.... מה בין גיטין ומה בין שבת? אמר רבי אבא: בשבת כתיב: לא תעשה מלאכה; נעשית היא מאיליה? ברם הכא: ונתן בידה - ברשותה.

משנה בבא קמא ד:ו

שור שהיה מתחכך בכתל ונפל על האדם: נתכון להרוג את הבהמה והרג את האדם; לנכרי והרג בן ישראל; לנפלים והרג בן קימא - פטור.

ותיק עתיד להורות לפני רבו כבר נאמר למשה בסיני. מה טעמא?
יש דבר שיאמר ראה זה חדש הוא! חבירו משיבו ואומר לו: כבר
היה לעולמים אשר היה לפנינו.

ירושלמי נדרים ג:ב

שוא ושקר - שניהם נאמרו בדיבור אחד מה שאי אפשר לפה לומר
ולא לאוזן לשמוע. זכור ושמור - שניהם בדיבור אחד נאמרו מה
שאי אפשר לפה לומר ולא לאוזן לשמוע....
וכן הוא אומר: אחת דיבר אלהים - בדיבור - שתים זו שמענו.
וכתיב: הלא כה דברי כאש נאם ה' וכפטיש יפוצץ סלע.

משנה סנהדרין ז:ח

המחלל את השבת - בדבר שחייבין על זדונו כרת ועל שגגתו
חטאת. המקלל אביו ואמו אינו חייב עד שיקללם בשם. קללם
בכנוי - רבי מאיר מחייב וחכמים פוטרין.

ירושלמי סנהדרין ז:יא

אזהרא למחלל מניין? לא תעשה כל מלאכה. כרת מניין? כי כל
העושה בו מלאכה ונכרתה. עונש מניין? מחלליה מות יומת....
אזהרה למקלל אביו ואמו מניין? איש אמו ואביו תיראו. עונש
וכרת מניין? ומקלל אביו ואמו מות יומת. ואומר: כי כל אשר
יעשה מכל התועבות האלה ונכרתה.

ירושלמי סנהדרין ח:ג

אזהרה לגניבה הראשונה מניין? לא תגנוב. אזהרה לגניבה שנייה
מניין? לא תגנובו. לא תגנובו על מנת למקט. לא תגנובו על מנת
לשלם תשלומי כפל על מנת לשלם תשלומי ארבעה וחמשה. בן בג
בג אומר: לא תגנוב את שלך מאחר הגנב שלא תראה גונג.

תחמוד בית רעך - וכתבתם על מזוזות ביתך; ביתך ולא בית
חבירך.

ירושלמי ברכות א:ה

תמן תנינן: אמר להם הממונה: ברכו ברכה אחת והן בירכו. מה
בירכו? רב מתנא אמר בשם שמואל: זו ברכת תורה. וקראו
עשרת הדברים, שמע, והיה אם שמוע, ויאמר. רבי אמי בשם רבי
לוי: זאת אומרת שאין הברכות מעכבות. אמר רבי בא: אין מן
הדא! לית את שמע מינה כלום שעשרת הדברות הן הן גופה של
שמע. דרב מתנא ורבי שמואל בר נחמן תרווייהון אמרי: בדין היה
שיהיו קורין עשרת הדברות בכל יום ומפני מה אין קורין אותן?
מפני טענות המינין שלא יהו אימרים: אלו לבדן ניתנו לו למשה
בסיני.

משנה כתובות ז:ו

ואלו יוצאות שלא בכתובה: העוברת על דת משה ויהודית. ואיזו
היא דת משה? מאכילתו שאינו מעושר ומשמשתו נדה ולא קוצה
לה חלה ונודרת ואינה מקימת. ואיזוהי דת יהודית? יוצאה
וראשה פרוע וטווה בשוק ומדברת עם כל אדם. אבא שאול
אומר: אף המקללת יולדיו בפניו. רבי טרפון אומר: אף הקולנית.

משנה חגיגה א:ח

התר נדרים פורחין באויר ואין להם על מה שיסמכו. הלכות שבת
חגיגות ומעילות הרי הם כהררים התלוין בשערה שהן מקרא מעט
והלכות מרבות. הדינין והעבודות הטהרות והטמאות והעריות יש
להן על מה שיסמכו. הן הן גופי תורה.

ירושלמי חגיגה א:ח

אמר רבי יהושע בן לוי: עליהם - ועליהם; כל - ככל; דברים -
הדברים: מקרא ומשנה תלמוד הלכות ואגדות; אפילו מה שתלמיד

ירושלמי פאה א:א

רובו זכיות יורש גן עדן, רובו עבירות יורש גיהנם. היה מעויין?

אמר רבי יוסי בן חנינא: נושא עונות אין כתיב כאן אלא נושא עון.

הקדוש ברוך הוא חוטף שטר אחד מן העבירות והזכיות מכריעות.

אמר רבי אלעזר: ולך אדני חסד כי אתה תשלם לאיש כמעשהו,

ואי לית ליה את יהיב ליה מן דידך. היא דעתיה דרבי אלעזר, דרבי

אלעזר אומר: ורב חסד - מתה כלפי חסד.

ירושלמי ברכות א:ה

מפני מה קורין שתי פרשיות הללו בכל יום? רבי לוי ורבי סימון.

רבי סימון אמר: מפני שכתוב בהן שכיבה וקימה. רבי לוי אמר:

מפני שעשרת הדברות כלולין בהן. אנכי ה׳ אלהיך - שמע ישראל

ה׳ אלהינו. לא יהיה לך אלהים אחרים על פני - ה׳ אחד. לא

תשא את שם ה׳ אלהיך לשוא - ואהבת את ה׳ אלהיך; מאן

דרחים מלכא לא משתבע בשמיה ומשקר. זכור את יום השבת

לקדשו - למען תזכרו; רבי אומר: זו מצות שבת שהיא שקולה

כנגד כל מצותיה של תורה, דכתיב: ואת שבת קדשך הודעת להם

ומצות וחוקים ותורה צוית וגו׳ להודיעך שהיא שקולה כנגד כל

מצותיה של תורה. כבד את אביך ואת אמך - למען ירבו ימיכם

וימי בניכם. לא תרצח - ואבדתם מהרה; מאן דקטיל מתקטיל.

לא תנאף - לא תתורו אחרי לבבכם ואחרי עיניכם; אמר רבי לוי:

ליבא ועינא תרין סרסורין דחטאה, דכתיב: תנה בני לבך לי ועיניך

דרכי תצרנה. אמר הקדוש ברוך הוא: אי יהבת לי לבך ועיניך אנא

ידע דאת לי. לא תגנוב - ואספת דגנך; ולא דגנו של חבירך. לא

תענה ברעך עד שקר אני ה׳ אלהיכם - וכתיב והי׳ אלהיכם אמת;

מהו אמת? אמר רבי אבון: שהוא אלהים חיים ומלך עולם. אמר

רבי לוי: אמר הקדוש ברוך הוא: אם העדת לחבירך עדות שקר

מעלה אני עליך כאלו העדת עלי שלא בראתי שמים וארץ. לא

Appendix: Talmudic Texts

Bibliography

Baker, D. L. *Two Testaments, One Bible: A Study of Some Modern Solutions to the Theological Problem of the Relationship of the Old and New Testaments.* Leicester, England: Inter-Varsity Press, 1976.

Barr, James. *The Bible in the Modern World.* San Francisco, Calif.: Harper & Row, 1973.

Berkovits, Eliezer. *Not in Heaven: On the Nature and Function of Halakhah.* New York: Ktav, 1983.

Boadt, Lawrence. *Reading the Old Testament: An Introduction.* New York: Paulist Press, 1984.

Bokser, Baruch M. "An Annotated Bibliographical Guide to the Study of the Palestinian Talmud." In Jacob Neusner, ed., *The Study of Ancient Judaism.* Vol. 2, *The Palestinian and Babylonian Talmuds,* pp. 1–119. New York: Ktav, 1981.

———. *Post Mishnaic Judaism in Transition: Samuel on Berakhot and the Beginnings of Gemara.* Brown Judaic Studies 17. Chico, Calif.: Scholars Press, 1980.

———. *The Origins of the Seder: The Passover Rite and Early Rabbinic Judaism.* Berkeley: University of California Press, 1984.

Borowitz, Eugene B. "Autonomy and Its Limits." In *Reform Judaism Today.* Vol. 3, *How We Live.* New York: Behrman House, 1978.

Brams, Steven J. *Biblical Games: A Strategic Analysis of Stories in the Old Testament.* Cambridge, Mass.: The MIT Press, 1980.

Bright, John. *A History of Israel.* 3d ed. Philadelphia, Pa.: Westminster Press, 1981.

Broad, C. D. *Five Types of Ethical Theory.* London: Routledge and Kegan Paul, 1956. Originally published 1930.

Brooks, Roger. "Judaism in Crisis? Institutions and Systematic Theology in Rabbinism." In Jacob Neusner, Ernest S. Frerichs, and Nahum M. Sarna, eds., *From Ancient Israel to Modern Judaism: Intellect in Quest of Understanding: Essays in Honor of Marvin Fox,* vol. 2, pp. 3–18. Atlanta, Ga.: Scholars Press, 1990.

———. *The Talmud of the Land of Israel: A Preliminary Translation and Commentary.* Vol. 2, *Tractate Peah.* Chicago, Ill.: University of Chicago Press, 1990.

Cassuto, Umberto, *La Questione della Genesi*. Florence: Publicazioni della R. Università degli Studi di Firenze. Facoltà di Lettere e Filosofia, 3d series, vol. 1, 1934. Revised and issued as *The Documentary Hypothesis and the Composition of the Pentateuch*. Jerusalem: Magnes Press, 1961. Originally published in Hebrew, 1941.

Charles, R. H. *The Decalogue*. Edinburgh: T. and T. Clark, 1923.

Childs, Brevard S. *Introduction to the Old Testament as Scripture*. Philadelphia, Pa.: Fortress Press, 1979.

Eilberg-Schwartz, Howard. *The Human Will in Judaism: The Mishnah's Philosophy of Intention*. Brown Judaic Studies 103. Atlanta, Ga.: Scholars Press, 1986.

Feldman, David M. *Marital Relations, Birth Control, and Abortion in Jewish Law: An Examination of the Rabbinic Legal Tradition that Underlies Jewish Values with Regard to Marriage, Sex, and Procreation, with Comparative Reference to Christian Tradition*. New York: Schocken Books, 1978. Originally published 1968.

Furnish, Victor Paul. *Theology and Ethics in Paul*. Nashville, Tenn.: Abingdon, 1968.

Gager, John G. *The Origins of Anti-Semitism: Attitudes toward Judaism in Pagan and Christian Antiquity*. New York: Oxford University Press, 1983.

Ginzburg, Louis. "Introductory Essay: The Palestinian Talmud." In Louis Ginzburg, *A Commentary on the Palestinian Talmud: A Study of the Development of the Halakhah and Haggadah in Palestine and Babylonia*. 4 vols. New York: Ktav, 1971. Originally published 1941.

Goldberg, Michael. *Jews and Christians: Getting Our Stories Straight: The Exodus and the Passion-Resurrection*. Nashville, Tenn.: Abingdon, 1985.

Goldin, Judah. *Studies in Midrash and Related Literature*. Philadelphia, Pa.: Jewish Publication Society, 1988.

Greenberg, Moshe. *Jewish Biblical Hermeneutics: Introductory Essays* (Hebrew). Jerusalem: Bialik, 1983.

Greer, Rowan A., ed. *Origen*. Classics of Western Spirituality. New York: Paulist Press, 1979.

Hahn, Herbert F. *The Old Testament in Modern Research: With a Survey of Recent Literature by Horace D. Hummel*. Philadelphia, Pa.: Fortress Press, 1966.

Halivni, David Weiss. *Midrash, Mishnah, and Gemara: The Jewish Predilection for Justified Law*. Cambridge, Mass.: Harvard University Press, 1986.

Hartmann, David. *A Living Covenant: The Innovative Spirit in Traditional Judaism.* New York: Free Press, 1985.

Heilman, Samuel C. *Synagogue Life: A Study in Symbolic Interaction.* Chicago, Ill.: University of Chicago Press, 1973.

Hertz, Joseph H. *The Authorized Daily Prayer Book: Hebrew Text, English Translation, with Commentary and Notes.* Rev. ed. New York: Bloch Publishers, 1985. Originally published 1948.

Heschel, Abraham Joshua. *God in Search of Man: A Philosophy of Judaism.* New York: Farrar, Strauss, and Giroux, 1955.

————. *The Sabbath: Its Meaning for Modern Man.* New York: Farrar, Strauss, and Young, 1951.

Hoffman, Lawrence. *The Canonization of the Synagogue Liturgy.* Notre Dame, Ind.: University of Notre Dame Press, 1979.

Hooker, Morna Dorothy. *New Wine in Old Bottles: A Discussion of Continuity and Discontinuity in Relation to Judaism and the Gospels.* The 1984 Ethel M. Wood Trust Lecture. London: London University Press, 1984.

Horowitz, H. S., and Y. A. Rabin, *Mekhilta de-Rabbi Yishmael: With Variant Readings and Notes.* 2d ed. Jerusalem: Wahrmann, 1960.

Hyman, Aaron. *Torah Ha-kᵊtuvah vᵊ-Ha-mᵊsurah: A Reference Book of the Scriptural Passages Quoted in Talmudic, Midrashic, and Early Rabbinic Literature.* 2d ed., rev. and enlarged by Arthur B. Hyman. 3 vols. Tel-Aviv: Dᵊvir Publishing, 1979.

ibn Yiḥyah, Gedaliah. *Shalshelet ha-Kabbalah.* Warsau: 1890. Originally published c. 1570.

Jacobs, Louis. *The Talmudic Argument: A Study in Talmudic Reasoning and Methodology.* Cambridge: Cambridge University Press, 1984.

Jewish Publication Society. *TANAKH: The Holy Scriptures: The New JPS Translation according to the Traditional Hebrew Text.* Philadelphia, Pa.: Jewish Publication Society, 1988.

Jonsen, Albert R., and Stephen Toulmin, *The Abuse of Casuistry.* Berkeley: University of California Press, 1988.

Lauterbach, Jacob Z. *Mekilta de-Rabbi Ishmael: A Critical Edition on the Basis of the Manuscripts and Early Editions with an English Translation, Introduction, and Notes.* 3 vols. Philadelphia, Pa.: Jewish Publication Society, 1933–1935.

Levenson, Jon D. *Sinai and Zion: An Entry into the Jewish Bible.* Minneapolis, Minn.: Winston Press, 1985.

Lewin, Benjamin Menasseh. *Iggeret Rav Sherirah Gaon in der franzöischen und spanischen Version.* Haifa: Godah-Ittskovski, 1921.

Lichtenstein, Aharon."Does Jewish Tradition Recognize an Ethic Independent of *Halakhah?*" In Menachem Marc Kellner, ed., *Contemporary Jewish Ethics.* New York: Sanhedrin Press, 1978.

Little, David, and Sumner B. Twiss, *Comparative Religious Ethics: A New Method*. San Francisco, Calif.: Harper & Row, 1978.

Montefiore, Claude Goldsmid. *Judaism and St. Paul: Two Essays*. New York: Arno Press, 1973. Originally published 1914.

Montesquieu, Charles Secondat. *The Spirit of the Laws*. English translation by Thomas Nugent. New York: Hafner Press, 1949. Originally published 1748.

Moore, George Foot. "Christian Writers on Judaism." In *Harvard Theological Review* 14, no. 3 (1921): 197–254.

Neusner, Jacob. "The Absoluteness of Christianity and the Uniqueness of Judaism." In *Interpretation: A Journal of Bible and Theology* 43, no. 1 (1989): 27–28.

———. *Aphrahat and Judaism: The Christian-Jewish Argument in Fourth-Century Iran*. Leiden: E. J. Brill, 1971.

———. *Comparative Midrash: The Plan and Program of Genesis and Leviticus Rabbah*. Atlanta, Ga.: Scholars Press, 1986.

———. *Invitation to Midrash: A Teaching Book: The Workings of Rabbinic Bible Interpretation*. San Francisco, Calif.: Harper & Row, 1989.

———. *Invitation to the Talmud: A Teaching Book*. Rev. and expanded ed. San Francisco, Calif.: Harper & Row, 1984. Originally published 1973.

———. *Judaism: The Classical Statement: The Evidence of the Bavli*. Chicago, Ill.: University of Chicago Press, 1986.

———. *Judaism: The Evidence of the Mishnah*. Chicago, Ill.: University of Chicago Press, 1981.

———. *Judaism and Scripture: The Evidence of Leviticus Rabbah*. Chicago, Ill.: University of Chicago Press, 1986.

———. *Judaism in Society: The Evidence of the Yerushalmi: Toward the Natural History of a Religion*. Chicago, Ill.: University of Chicago Press, 1983.

———. *Mekhilta according to Rabbi Ishmael. An Analytic Translation*. 2 vols. Atlanta, Ga.: Scholars Press, 1988.

———. *Mekhilta according to Rabbi Ishmael: An Introduction to Judaism's First Scriptural Encyclopaedia*. Atlanta, Ga.: Scholars Press, 1988.

———. *Messiah in Context: The Foundations of Judaism: Method, Teleology, Doctrine*. Philadelphia, Pa.: Fortress, 1984.

———. *Method and Meaning in Ancient Judaism*. 3d series. Chico, Calif.: Scholars Press, 1981.

———. *Sifra: An Analytic Translation*. 3 vols. Brown Judaic Studies 138, 139, and 140. Atlanta, Ga.: Scholars Press, 1988.

——. *The Enchantments of Judaism: Rites of Transformation from Birth through Death.* New York: Basic Books, 1987.

——. *The Mishnah: A New Translation.* New Haven, Conn.: Yale University Press, 1988.

Neusner, Jacob, ed. *The Study of Ancient Judaism.* Vol. 2, *The Palestinian and Babylonian Talmuds.* New York: Ktav, 1981.

Neusner, Jacob, et al. *The Talmud of the Land of Israel: A Preliminary Translation and Explanation.* 35 vols. Chicago, Ill.: University of Chicago Press, 1983–

Newman, Louis E. *The Sanctity of the Seventh Year: A Study of Mishnah Tractate Shebiit.* Brown Judaic Studies 44. Chico, Calif.: Scholars Press, 1983.

Novak, David. *Halakhah in a Theological Dimension.* Brown Judaic Studies 68. Chico, Calif.: Scholars Press, 1985.

Rendtorff, Rolf. "The Image of Post-Exilic Israel in German Bible Scholarship from Wellhausen to von Rad." Delivered at the 1988 Annual Meeting of the Society of Biblical Literature, Chicago, Illinois.

——. *The Old Testament: An Introduction.* Philadelphia, Pa.: Fortress Press, 1985. Originally published in German, 1983.

Rosenzweig, Franz. *The Star of Redemption.* English translation of the 2d ed. of 1930 by William W. Hallo. Notre Dame, Ind.: University of Notre Dame Press, 1985.

Rosner, Fred. *Moses Maimonides' Commentary on the Mishnah: Introduction to Seder Zeraim and Commentary on Tractate Berakhot. English translation with notes and general introduction.* New York: Feldheim Publishers, 1975.

Sanders, E. P. *Paul and Palestinian Judaism: A Comparison of Patterns of Religion.* Philadelphia, Pa.: Fortress Press, 1977.

——. *Paul, the Law, and the Jewish People.* Philadelphia, Pa.: Fortress Press, 1983.

Sarna, Nahum M. *Exploring Exodus: The Heritage of Biblical Israel.* New York: Schocken Books, 1986.

Schechter, Solomon. "The Law and Recent Criticism." In *Studies in Judaism.* 1st series. Philadelphia, Pa.: Jewish Publication Society, 1938.

Schwab, Moise. *Le Talmud de Jérusalem.* 6 vols. Paris: G.P. Maisonneuve, 1960.

Shereshevsky, Esra. *Rashi: The Man and His Life.* New York: Sepher-Hermon Press, 1982.

Simon, Marcel. *Verus Israel: A Study of the Relationships between Christians and Jews in the Roman Empire.* New York: Oxford, 1986. Originally published in French, 1948.

Soloveitchik, Joseph B. *Halakhic Man.* Philadelphia, Pa.: Jewish Publication Society, 1983. Originally published in Hebrew, 1944.

Steinsaltz, Adin. *The Essential Talmud.* New York: Bantam Books, 1976. Originally published in Hebrew.

————. *The Talmud Yerushalmi: Tractate Peah. Explained, Translated, and Pointed.* Hebrew. Jerusalem: The Israel Institute for Talmudic Publications, 1987.

Stern, David. "Midrash and Indeterminacy." In *Criticial Inquiry* 15, no. 1 (Autumn 1988): 132–61.

Strack, Hermann L. *Einleitung in Talmud und Midrasch,* Rev. and edited by Günter Stemberger. Munich: C. H. Beck, 1982.

van der Heide, A. "PARDES: Methodological Reflections on the Theory of the Four Senses." In *Journal of Jewish Studies* 35, no. 2 (1983): 147–59.

Vanhoye, Albert. *Old Testament Priests and the New Priest, According to the New Testament.* Petersham, Mass.: St. Bede's Publications, 1986. Originally published in French, 1980.

Wellhausen, Julius. *Prolegomenon to the History of Ancient Israel. With a Reprint of the Article "Israel", from the Encyclopedia Britannica. Preface by W. Robertson Smith.* Gloucester, Mass.: Peter Smith Publisher, 1973. Originally published 1886.

Wilde, Robert, *The Treatment of the Jews in the Greek Christian Writers of the First Three Centuries.* Washington, D.C.: Catholic University of America Press, 1949.

Wilken, Robert L. *John Chrysostom and the Jews: Rhetoric and Reality in the Late Fourth Century.* Berkeley: University of California Press, 1983.

————. *The Christians as the Romans Saw Them.* New Haven, Conn.: Yale University Press, 1984.

Index to the Ten Commandments

Index of Scriptural and Talmudic Passages

Index of Topics

---

* The dates within parentheses refer to the years in which the Rabbi flourished.